A Journal of Israel's Betrayal

TRAITORS

AND

CARPETBAGGERS

IN THE PROMISED LAND

BARRY CHAMISH

Hearthstone Publishing
Oklahoma City, Oklahoma

Published by:
Hearthstone Publishing
4805 NW 10th St. ▪ Oklahoma City, OK 73127
(405) 946-7050 ▪ (800) 580-2604 ▪ FAX (405) 946-8898

ISBN 1-57558-017-9

Table of Contents

Chapter Five

Chapter Six

Acknowledgments

Inside Israel could not have existed without Joel Bainerman, who cofounded and then coedited the newsletter for four years. Without our special chemistry, the veil of secrecy would not have been lifted.

When *Inside Israel* was initiated, Joel and I fully expected that our subscribers would be concerned Jews yearning for reform in Israel. In fact, we were quickly shunned by the mainstream Jewish decision makers and embraced by two wonderful groups, neither of which we belong to—Orthodox Jews and Christian Zionists.

The Orthodox Jews took their time in recognizing that *Inside Israel* was reflecting their fears about the hidden machinations of the Israeli government. Today they comprise the majority of our advocates. But to our utter surprise, it was initially Christians who were our most ardent supporters. Unintentionally, our research verified their prophecies and world view.

We were at a loss to explain why, but our Christian friends had a much better grasp of what was happening to Israel, or more correctly, what was being done to Israel. I came to know them, admire their way of living, their decency and, to me anyway, their perplexing, heartfelt concern for the survival of the Jewish state.

I thank them all; Chris Barder who published *Inside Israel* from England for three years; and those wonderful Jerusalemites, Jew and Christian, who attended my lectures, subscribed faithfully to my newsletter, invited me to their homes, donated to my work, offered vital moral support, and yes, prayed for me; Gemma, Hannah, Lilly, Leah, Yael, Kent, Bradley, David, Arnold, Marilyn, Hanoch, Menachem, Marianne, and so many more.

Of the many, one person deserves special recognition for her intelligence, initiative, and intuition—Carol Rushton, who thought this book had to be read widely and did something about it.

May our reward be the kind of country Israel was destined to be.

Foreword

From Deuteronomy 28 to Revelation 22, the dispersion of Israel into all nations for two thousand years was prophesied. In accordance with Isaiah 66, and hundreds of other scriptures, Israel became a nation once more on May 14, 1948.

The rebuilding of a desolate land into the biblical land of promise, flowing with milk and honey, has been a mission of dedication, commitment, and faith by the returning remnant. But as it was when the remnant returned after the Babylonian captivity period, the rebuilding process has proceeded while struggling against enemies from without and traitors from within.

A parallel can also be drawn to the condition of the southern states after the Civil War. The South was in a state of shock and economic chaos while lamenting its dead. A group of unscrupulous political and financial profiteers came down from the North, bringing with them their sole possessions in carpet bags. The carpetbaggers joined with Southern scalawags (traitors). This unholy union resulted in the worse type of political and economic governmental corruption.

Most Americans, and especially evangelical Christians, hope and pray for nothing but the best for Israel and its citizens. However, like most Israelis today, we are appalled at the perversion of the biblical promises into a quagmire of deception, intrigue, frustration, and financial advantage.

This little land, only seventy-five miles wide at its widest point, and barely over three hundred miles long, is indeed the most valuable piece of real estate in the world. So, in have come the foreign carpetbaggers—political, financial, religious—to join with Israeli scalawags (traitors), bringing to doubt the very future existence of this nation as a homeland for the Jews.

This book will be a challenge to the reader. The continuous parade of names, places, and dates will tax the attention span. However, these same names, places, and dates also serve as documentation to the credibility of that account set forth by the author. In any event, you are going to read things about the contemporary affairs of Israel that you have never read in newspapers or seen on television. Yet, these very things about which the author reports are the biblical birth-pangs which must precede the messianic age.

—N. W. Hutchings

Chapter One

The Shaky Foundations of Rabin's Government

Contrary to the way the international media presented the Israeli elections, the public did not "vote for peace." The 61–59 split in favor of the left was only possible because Israeli Arabs voted for Zionist parties and the new Russian immigrants issued a strong protest vote against the previous government.

To form a majority government, it was incumbent upon Prime Minister Yitzhak Rabin to lure at least one of the religious parties into the coalition. Had the three religious parties closed ranks, they would have had enough seats to prevent Rabin from forming a majority government.

Shas is part of that haredi (ultra-Orthodox) bloc. A deal was cut with Shas, and their Knesset leader, Arye Deri—who has been under police investigation for fraud and embezzlement since mid-1990—to remain as interior minister. Numerous other Shas members are being investigated for crimes, including Rabin's new communications minister, Raphael Pinchasi, who is strongly suspected of electioneering fraud.

Three days before Shas agreed to enter the coalition, the FBI announced it was investigating Deri for illegally transferring money to the U.S. and for possible complicity in the death of his wife's adoptive mother.

Did Rabin make a deal with Deri whereby he would enter the coalition in exchange for quashing the police investigation? As soon as Labor was elected, Attorney-General Yosef Harish sent a letter to Rabin recommending that Deri be kept out of the government. Rabin ignored the warning and instead appointed David Libai, Haim Ramon, and Moshe Shachal to come up with a formula whereby if Harish found enough evidence to warrant a prosecution, Deri would voluntarily "suspend" himself from the government until after his trial. Rabin called the plan "a new precedent in government reform" when in fact suspension meant Deri would still remain a government minister and immune from prosecution. The Knesset would have to pass a law lifting immunity before any court could try him.

Yediot Achronot said the arrangement "stunk" and that "it would haunt Rabin for years." Hadashot noted that "when Moshe Shachal is in a room, there's bound to be a lie told."

The most puzzling aspect of the whole affair is that between the time the deal was made and the opening of the Knesset on July 13, 1992, Deri was reported to have taken a mysterious two-day trip to Morocco. Yet just before being sworn in as interior minister in Rabin's government, he told a *Maariv* reporter: "I'm not allowed to speak about this. It is a sensitive, secret matter and publicizing the visit would be damaging" (to whom he didn't disclose).

Shachal was soon after appointed police minister and Libai minister of justice. Only the police minister can quash an ongoing police investigation; the justice minister has the authority to prevent a case from going to trial.

Deri truly has friends in high places.

Secrets of Kennebunkport

It's believed that since April 1990 Prime Minister Shamir's office had been compiling files on President Bush's involvement in Iran-Contra. Those dossiers are now safely in the hands of Rabin's office and Bush must be breathing a sigh of relief.

Shortly after the recent Israeli elections, Yitzhak Shamir wrote a letter to President Bush formally asking him to try to seek Jonathan Pollard's release. The timing of the request wasn't coincidental. Although the letter was widely reported in Israel, it never became an issue in America. Had it, it might have put Bush into a position where he would have been pressed to act.

One of the reasons why Rabin escaped unscathed from the Pollard scandal, which occurred while he was defense minister in 1985, may have been due to his vast knowledge of Bush's role in Iran-Contra, specifically his meeting with then-Prime Minister Shimon Peres' counterterrorism adviser Amiram Nir at the King David Hotel in July 1986. Rabin's aides admitted to the Israeli press that Pollard was discussed at Kennebunkport, but gave no details. Did Bush give Rabin an assurance at Kennebunkport that to keep Rabin's role in the scandal secret Pollard wouldn't be released?

The granting of the loan guarantees won Bush a few points in the Jewish community. However, he might have been given a helping hand by Rabin. During Rabin's visit to the U.S., it was revealed that Hillary Clinton was a director of the New World Fund which contributed to Palestinian organizations tied to the PLO. Despite Rabin's statements that "Israel will in no way interfere with the American election," the Israeli prime minister may have tried to do just that. Bush and Rabin also discussed the "new era in strategic Israeli-American cooperation." Just days after Rabin's victory, one of President Bush's most trusted aides, former Assistant Secretary of Defense Richard Armitage, proposed joint Israeli-American aid projects for the CIS's Moslem republics of Uzbekistan, Kazakhstan, Kirgizastan, Turkemenstan, and Tadzhikstan. More than $4 million has been allocated for the first stage of the "program."

During his trip Rabin was asked by Indiana Democrat Lee Hamilton to allow certain Israeli individuals to testify before a congressional investigating team to determine whether the Reagan campaign team in 1980 conspired to delay the release of the U.S. hostages held in Iran. Rabin refused. If these charges have no basis in fact, why is Rabin so adamant in his refusal to allow Israeli officials to testify and help put the conspiracy theories to rest once and for all?

With Rabin heading the Israeli government, and serving as both prime minister and defense minister, highly secret information on joint U.S.-Israel covert initiatives will have to pass by his desk first.

President Bush can breathe more easily.

February 1993

Rabin's Peres Problem

The chronology of Shimon Peres' attempt to overthrow Yitzhak Rabin's approach to the regional peace talks began on September 10, 1992, with meetings in Paris with French foreign minister Roland Dumas and President Francois Mitterand. Peres, whose ties to France date from his arms purchasing days in the 1950s, invited the French, whom Rabin dislikes, to act as intermediaries in the multilateral peace negotiations.

They accepted the invitation enthusiastically and before Peres left France, Syria had agreed to direct meetings between Peres and his Syrian counterpart, Farouk Shara. In response to this break-through, Peres spoke of Syria's "sensational" change of attitude toward Israel.

Rabin met Peres at Ben Gurion Airport on his return and tried to put an end to his policy finagling, even referring to the French as "the biggest bastards." Nonetheless, on September 14 Dumas landed in Damascus to promote whatever plan had been agreed to four days previously. This was stage one of a shuttle that took him to Cairo and back to Damascus.

By November Peres was in Cairo meeting with Egyptian president Hosni Mubarak. Once again Peres made a strong impression, causing the Egyptian foreign minister, Omar Moussa, to make an urgent visit to Jerusalem shortly after with a plan for a break-through in the stalled peace talks.

His trip did not go well and the only result was a very minor Israeli municipal concession to the Palestinians. At the closing press conference, the Egyptian diplomat even refused a three-way handshake between him, Peres, and Rabin.

In early December it was Mitterand's turn to visit Israel and his trip was no less a fiasco. Clearly peeved, Mitterand insisted that Israel negotiate with the PLO. By doing so, he earned Rabin's ire and cancellation of a courtesy call to former prime minister Yitzhak Shamir.

Following the visit, Peres vowed not to interfere with Rabin's foreign policy. Peres' efforts resulted in Egyptian foreign minister Omar Moussa visiting Israel, an exceedingly rare occurrence, and Syria agreeing to negotiations at the Foreign Ministry level, which was previously viewed as a near impossibility. These were no mean accomplishments, but led to a dead end.

What could Peres have offered Syria and Egypt?

The answer may lie in leaks from Peres' meeting with Mubarak. According to reliable Foreign Ministry officials, Mubarak discussed changing the terms of the Camp David Accords with Peres. The Egyptian leader wants all foreign troops, including those Americans manning listening posts, removed from the Sinai.

His plan calls for remilitarization of half the Sinai with Egyptian troops. To assure no double-dealing, Israeli jets would be allowed overflight privileges in return for reciprocal Egyptian flights over the Negev.

What shocked the Israeli diplomats was Peres' agreement to present the plan to the Israeli government. By not rejecting the proposed reneging on the Camp David Accords, Egypt was sufficiently encouraged to send its foreign minister flying to Jerusalem.

The Israelis were told that the threat of fundamentalism to the Egyptian regime is real and can only be appeased by the removal of foreign troops from its soil. But the hand of Syria seemed to be in the proposal.

If Syria and Israel do come up with an agreement, it will certainly mean the stationing of American troops on the Golan Heights. President Assad will not tolerate armed Americans on Syrian territory under any circumstances. He hoped that the removal of American troops from the Sinai would wipe out the Camp David precedent.

The French would be very pleased to see American influence reduced in the Middle East and theirs increased, and felt Peres was the ideal vehicle for their designs; hence their backing for a most unlikely basis for a Middle East breakthrough.

Awash in Easy Money

Although Israel's foreign debt stands at $24.5 billion and increased by only $82 million since December 1991, that might change drastically in the near future.

Israel will pay a stiff price for the $10 billion in loan guarantees recently approved by the U.S. Senate. In addition to the high cost of the loans, economists in Israel are now doubting whether the assistance is even needed.

The loans will be paid back over thirty years. In the tenth year Israel will begin to pay back the principal and interest. The interest will be 7 percent a year, in addition to the 3.5 percent risk factor premium. If Israel takes the full $10 billion over the next five years, from the eleventh year until the thirtieth year it will have to pay interest of $700 million a year (on the $10 billion), $50 million in risk insurance, and $100 million in principal. This would be $1.2 billion a year, in 1992 dollars.

March 1993

The editors believe the following was one of the most important revelations. Inside Israel *revealed the secret dealings in Oslo seven months before they were made public.*

Talking with the PLO

Prime Minister Yitzhak Rabin may have relented to demands by members of his own party to open a dialogue with the PLO.

According to the Lebanese publication *El-Kifach Al El Arabi,* unofficial secret talks are underway between PLO officials aligned with Yasser Arafat and the Israeli government in a number of European capitals, including London and Paris. The PLO representatives, it is believed, are trying to convince the Rabin government that Arafat is serious about his intentions to reach a peace treaty with Israel.

The French magazine *Le Canard Enchaine* reveals that French experts will establish a Palestinian police force to secure an autonomy arrangement in the West Bank and Gaza. The publication stated that the agreement was reached during a series of meetings in November 1992 in London under the auspices of the American government.

It is believed that the two sides agreed on three principal points: the French will be responsible for establishing a local Palestinian police force; the force will be able to mobilize hundreds of Palestinians who live in the territories for active service; and it will be accountable, on an interim basis, to the Israel Defense Forces.

The magazine further states that Arafat's control over the PLO has been put in jeopardy by the secret meetings.

Sources in Israel say one of the reasons the talks are continuing in secret is because Israel wants to conclude an agreement with the PLO before the negotiations are made public. Some Israeli government officials are opposed to the initiative and are credited with leaking details of the meetings to the European and Arab press.

April 1993

Was Syria Behind the Buenos Aires Blast?

Although it has been two years since the bombing of the Israeli Embassy in Buenos Aires which left twenty-six dead and two hundred people injured, no one has yet been apprehended. Just days after the blast, the Argentinian news agency Telam reported that four men and a woman had been arrested by the Federal Police Anti-terrorist Brigade in a raid on a downtown apartment. The Argentinian police said the raid was connected to the bombing, but gave no further details. The police's press office subsequently denied the report.

The initial investigation was delayed five and one-half hours after the blast, by which time much of the evidence had been destroyed in the rescue operation. The official investigation has now been frozen, though the latest theory is that the explosion occurred in the basement of the embassy compound, indirectly implicating the Israelis in storing weapons which accidentally exploded.

This directly contradicts the evidence of a suicide bomber. Body parts belonging to a dark-skinned man flew through the window of a doctor living close to the embassy. Ballistics experts said the force required for these body parts to have been hurled through the window strongly suggests a suicide bomber. Several other corpses remain unidentified to this day.

Israeli investigators arrived just after the blast. They found the remains of a car inside the embassy compound and traced it to a Pakistani named Abbas Malek who was the personal aide to the Pakistani ambassador. Malek was filmed escaping the blast site minutes after the explosion by Israeli Embassy cameras. Two top-ranking Argentinian intelligence officials were given access to the photographs. After the investigation was frozen, they leaked the license number of the photographed car to a local TV station's investigation.

Also caught on film was the license plate of the suicide vehicle. It was traced to a car dealer who admitted selling the car three weeks before the blast to an Arab with a Brazilian accent, Ribahru Dahloz, who paid him in cash. The dealer demanded a 30 percent commission, which he was paid partly in bank notes later deposited in Syrian banks. Even with this evidence the police did not attempt to apprehend Dahloz.

This was the first hint of a carefully concealed Syrian connection to the explosion. On the day of the blast, both police security guards normally posted outside the embassy were absent. According to the police, one guard was late, while the other was removed by the Israeli ambassador, Yitzhak Shefi—an accusation he vehemently denies. One of the guards previously spent six years working at the Syrian Embassy.

Argentinian president Carlos Menem was born in Syria. According to Israeli journalist Nurit Steinberg who is living in Buenos Aires and has investigated the bombing, Menem maintains close ties with members of terrorist groups within the Syrian community. Steinberg gathered dozens of documents confirming these connections and has published the findings of her investigation in the Jerusalem weekly *Kol Hair*, which is owned by the prestigious Hebrew daily newspaper *Haaretz*.

Her work, however, was not well received. She has been constantly threatened, had a grenade thrown at her doorstep, and had her house broken into. Only one object was stolen: the computer diskette of her investigation.

Menem's wife, Suliema, was born in the Syrian town of Yatrud, also the birthplace of Monzer Al-Kassar, a drug and arms smuggler who has been implicated in the PanAm flight 103 bombing and who also helped Oliver North supply weapons to the Nicaraguan Contras. Al-Kassar has built a multimillion dollar empire on military deals in Eastern and Western Europe. In July 1987, the *Los Angeles Times* reported that it was clear that Al-Kassar had business links with the Abu Nidal terrorist organization.

Nine months before the embassy blast, a television news report from Damascus showed Menem's brother Munir, at the time his country's ambassador to Syria, deep in conversation with Al-Kassar. Shortly after the bombing, he was recalled.

Six months after the attack on the embassy, Al-Kassar was finally apprehended in Spain and put on trial for smuggling explosives to terrorists. The Argentinian government requested his extradition, claiming he was wanted in Argentina for passport violations. At the trial Al-Kassar claimed he received his Argentinian passport directly from Menem and even posed for the photo wearing the president's tie.

The Spanish government followed the Argentinian request with an extradition order of their own. They wanted Menem's personal secretary, Amira Yuma, to stand trial for being a member of the biggest drug network in Spain. Yuma is Menem's sister-in-law. Argentina, not surprisingly, turned down the request.

In September 1992, Menem sent a message to Jerusalem asking that the Israeli ambassador to Argentina, Yitzhak Shefi, be recalled. Shefi had publicly attacked Menem, who still maintained that neo-Nazis were behind the bombing. Shefi also accused the Israeli government of not protesting the stalled investigation, adding that perhaps Jerusalem was not really interested in finding out who was behind the blast. He was amongst a chorus of people who claimed that the investigation was being delayed to prevent a major diplomatic embarrassment both for the Argentinians and the Israelis.

The blast had all the hallmarks of a classic Shiite car bombing. It is also difficult to ignore the timing of the attack. It occurred one month to the day after Israeli forces killed the Syrian-controlled Hizbollah leader, Abbas Musawi, and not long after the last of the American hostages were released from Lebanon.

Musawi had more enemies in America than in Israel. In the early 1980s he planned the attacks on the American Embassy in Beirut and the Marine barracks compound which left 241 servicemen dead. He is also widely believed to have ordered the kidnappings of Americans in Lebanon (including William Buckley,

CIA station chief in Beirut).

At a memorial service one year after the Buenos Aires blast, Israeli foreign minister Shimon Peres stated that Israel knew who was behind the terrorist act, but would not say who. Everyone assumed Peres meant Iran. However, the evidence points directly to Damascus.

Peres and the administration may be covering up for the Syrians in order not to embarrass Assad and jeopardize his role in the Middle East peace talks.

Why Labor Is So Generous to Shas

In a recent state comptroller report, it was revealed that the Labor Party made a secret deal with Shas in October 1989. In return for supporting Labor in the Histadrut (Labor Federation) elections, Shas was given more than a million dollars in public funds Labor had received from the treasury for its election campaign. According to Arye Deri, the bribe was offered to him by Industry and Trade Minister Micha Harish and Transportation Minister Yisrael Kessar. At the time, Harish was Labor Party chairman and Kessar was head of the Histadrut.

Yet the origins of Shas-Labor ties begin six years earlier in 1983 when Health Minister Haim Ramon, then a Labor member of Knesset, befriended the up-and-coming Arye Deri. Deri was flattered, even overwhelmed, by the attention and started sharing contacts with Ramon.

The best known Deri-Ramon associate is Moshe Reich, a 38-year-old American-born electronics importer. He was charged in 1991 with cheating the state of $7.9 million in unreported customs duties. A few months later the charge was lowered to $1.8 million and then dropped altogether, much to the outrage of the judge and prosecutor who strongly suspected political intervention.

Reich may yet have his day in court. He is under investigation for a $100,000 bribe to Deri which subsequently helped pay for the minister's luxury apartment at 228 Hakablan Street in Jerusalem. An FBI file on him remains open as well; he was driving a car which ran over Deri's mother-in-law, Esther Verdberger.

Ramon also benefited from Deri's introduction to Reich. While he was a sitting member of the Knesset, he was hired by Reich to act as attorney in the purchase of his mortgage bank, Yasur, and earned a commission in the mid-five figure range.

The weekly magazine *Haolam Hazeh* claims outright that Ramon was sent in 1983 to recruit Deri, and the reasoning is perfectly logical. The Moroccan community had twice voted en masse against Labor, in 1977 and 1981. By breaking up the Likud–Moroccan coalition, Peres, Ramon, and the Labor Party would rule again.

Shas is the party representing Moroccan interests, and Ramon is the member of the Knesset representing Shas's interest. It was he who pressed Prime Minister Rabin to accept Shas in favor of the United Torah Judaism (UTJ) list during the coalition building, and it is he who is continuing to antagonize the UTJ on behalf of Labor. Rabin is not totally unaware of Ramon's finagling and the issue has driven a noticeable wedge between them.

Also considered a key figure in the recruitment of Deri is police minister Moshe Shachal. According to the daily *Maariv*, the relationship between the two "is like father and son." In 1984 Shachal offered to pay Deri's tuition if he went to law school and promised him a position in his law firm.

Another major link between the Labor Party and Shas is Deputy Foreign Minister Yossi Beilin and his boss, Shimon Peres.

In March 1990, Shas bolted the Likud-led National Unity Government and the coalition fell after a no-confidence vote. The issue was whether or not to accept James Baker's five-point peace plan hatched in Cairo. Shas, without any significant foreign policy platform, and whose constituents are mostly on the right wing of the political spectrum, suddenly became a party of doves and sided with the Labor Party. Shas's supporters, feeling deeply betrayed, eventually forced the party to rejoin the Likud coalition. The question as to why Shas broke up the government over such an unlikely issue remains unanswered.

But two Jerusalem municipal politicians, city counselor Shmuel Meir and deputy mayor Ornan Yekutieli, think they know the reason. According to the two public servants, in October of 1989, six months previously, then-deputy finance minister Yossi Beilin bragged that he had Shas in his back pocket. "Shas," he said, "will stay bought this time."

Meir and Yekutieli describe a situation in which Beilin discovered substantial misappropriations at Deri's Interior Ministry. He allowed the theft to go on, recording each shekel, and then presented his findings to Deri.

If Beilin unilaterally permitted the misappropriation of tens of millions of dollars of public funds in order to blackmail a party, then according to legal expert Moshe Negbi, he was an accomplice in the crime, itself a criminal offense.

If, on the other hand, Beilin reported his discoveries to his superior, then-finance minister Shimon Peres, what was once simple persuasion comes closer to a silent *coup d'etat* based on blackmail and embezzlement. Did Foreign Minister Peres give Shas an ultimatum to bring down the government or face the legal consequences? Meir insists he did. "On the very eve of the no-confidence vote," he says, "I saw a letter from Peres in which he promised a certain religious organization a great deal of money."

Labor's ties to Shas will be revealed if Deri stands trial, and the interior minister has already warned that unless the investigation against him is completed, he will "reveal the the whole truth to the public."

Chapter Two

Inside Israel was the first publication in English to expose the secret deal Labor concocted with the PLO to rig the June 1992 elections.

June 1993

Beilin's Secret Diplomacy

In June 1991 Yossi Beilin, deputy to Labor Party leader Shimon Peres, led a delegation of six Labor MKs* to Cairo. He disappeared from his group for several hours without explanation. Had they known why, the other members might have questioned the real reason for their Egyptian junket, or protested it.

In fact, Beilin went to the King Hotel and there met two high-ranking PLO officials; Said Kamal, the PLO's representative in Cairo, and Mahmoud Abbas, a special envoy from Yasser Arafat. Beilin handed Abbas a written message from Peres. In it he asked the PLO leader to use his influence to persuade Israeli Arabs to vote en masse for Labor in the national elections scheduled for 1992. In return, if Labor was elected it would immediately freeze settlements in the administered territories, adopt a land-for-peace policy, and cancel the law prohibiting meetings between Israelis and members of the PLO.

The last promise is significant. Beilin and Peres were both well aware that the former's meeting with Kamal and Abbas was against Israeli law, which as MKs they were sworn to uphold. Peace activist Abie Nathan had already sat in prison for abrogating it. Nevertheless, Beilin was consorting with the enemy on orders from his superior.

To sweeten the offer, Beilin called a press conference and to-

* *Member of Knesset*

gether the MKs announced that they would act to make three changes in their party's platform: initiate a land-for-peace program; freeze settlements; and not so ironically, alter the law banning meetings with the PLO.

By January 1992 two things were becoming clear to Arafat: elections would be held later that year; and Shimon Peres would probably lose the party's leadership to Yitzhak Rabin. Egyptian president Hosni Mubarak sent a delegation to Jerusalem to find out if the Peres deal offered to Arafat would be valid if Rabin took over the party. Peres assured the Egyptians that nothing would change, though clearly he knew Rabin would never play along with secret deals with the PLO, whom he despised.

On January 17, Secretary of State James Baker met with Mubarak and told him that the United States government would begin a campaign to force Israel into freezing settlement expansion. This message was transmitted by the American ambassador to Egypt to Nabil Shaat, Arafat's diplomatic advisor.

Two days later Beilin was in Cairo on his second known "secret" mission. Unfortunately for him, he was spotted by Yehoshua Meiri, of the Hebrew daily *Hadashot,* entering the lobby of the Ramses Hilton Hotel. Meiri watched him enter a room, to be followed a few minutes later by Nabil Shaat.

Beilin's secret was out and two Egyptian newspapers, *Al-Gomhouriya* and *Al-Wafd,* disclosed details of the meeting. According to Shaat—who felt free to talk since Meiri had witnessed him with Beilin—Peres upped the stakes. If the PLO rallied Arab voters behind Labor, helping it to oust the Likud coalition from power, his government would support an "independent autonomous entity" led by the PLO, i.e., something resembling a Palestinian state.

Although a credible Cairo-based Israeli journalist had witnessed the meeting, Shaat had confirmed it, and two Egyptian papers had printed details of it, Beilin denied that it had ever taken place. Incredibly, the Israeli media missed the story. No connection was made with the Baker trip to Cairo two days earlier.

None of this was lost on the PLO, however. Shaat returned to Tunis with promises from the American secretary of state and the leader of the Israeli opposition that they would work toward a settlement freeze which would clear the way for something close to statehood. But not everyone accepted these promises unequivocally. While Shaat was satisfied with the assurances he had received, he was opposed by about half the PLO leadership which wanted something concrete before agreeing to work with Peres.

The skeptics won the day in February, after Rabin wrested Labor Party leadership from Peres. Rabin had been the defense minister during the first two and a half years of the intifada, and his measures to quell the uprising had earned him enemies in the PLO.

Arafat could not ignore the dissension in his ranks about supporting a party led by Rabin. Soon after Rabin's ascension, the PLO invited the Palestinian delegates to the peace talks and leaders of three radical Israeli political parties to Cairo. Arafat called for the delegates and the politicians to close ranks behind one united pro-PLO party. Arafat promised to deliver enough supporters to the polls to make unity worthwhile. But the politicians could not settle disagreements and the plan failed.

With the unity scheme unworkable, Arafat sent orders to local Arab town councils and village leaders to support Labor. On election day, June 23, Arab voters united behind Labor and made enough of a difference to change the government. Effectively, the PLO decided who was to run Israel. Now Arafat wanted his reward for his cooperation. As soon as Peres was appointed foreign minister and Beilin his deputy, he demanded that their promises to him be honored.

However, Rabin had different ideas. He felt the Israeli public had voted for him personally and not his dovish party. He accepted promoting a settlement freeze, but would neither change the basis of the peace talks nor permit a lifting of the PLO meetings ban.

In response, Mubarak sent a now infamous message to Rabin

demanding that he live up to commitments made by the party when Peres was the leader.

Rabin refused to budge. Again, on September 11, Beilin embarked on a trip to Cairo, this time for two days of top-level meetings. The issue this time was not how to conduct diplomacy behind the back of the Likud, but behind that of his own leader.

Predictably, the Americans pitched in. Prior to Beilin's arrival, President Bush's special emissary, Dennis Ross, sent a message to Arafat via Shaat promising a restoration of American relations if Israel cancelled its ban on meetings with the PLO. In response, Arafat's message to Beilin was that he wanted a change in the law before the American elections.

Beilin explained to the Egyptians that he couldn't deliver that quickly without challenging Rabin's leadership, which would have been political suicide. Mubarak asked Arafat to give Peres more time. Arafat adamantly refused and expressed his anger, along with some threats, in a letter given by Shaat to Beilin on September 12 and delivered to Peres that evening. The letter accused Peres of treachery and threatened to reveal the meetings with Beilin, which would have been viewed as treason in Israel. Further, Arafat would end the peace process and tie the PLO to the rejection front permanently.

Arafat lived up to his word and within a few weeks flew to Sudan to make his peace with the radicals, while Kamal Said leaked details of his own meetings with Beilin, stopping just short of naming him. Meanwhile, the Palestinian delegation was ordered by the PLO to create an aura of crisis and breakdown at the peace talks in Washington.

The Egyptians panicked and Mubarak sent Omar Moussa, his foreign minister, to Jerusalem to implore Rabin to live up to the promises Peres made to Arafat. To prod the prime minister, he sent a message; Mubarak was considering reneging on the Camp David Accords and placing armored units in half the Sinai Peninsula in contravention of the disarmament agreements. Even though Mubarak was threatening (not so subtly) a diplomatic war, Rabin would still not agree to Arafat's terms. Moussa returned to Cairo with an innocuous concession in the autonomy negotiations which expanded Palestinian municipal authority somewhat as a sop to the PLO leader.

Arafat was not appeased and pulled the joker out of the pack. He announced that he had no choice but to turn over PLO policy to the rejection front. Or, simply, he threatened to abandon diplomacy in favor of terrorism. Peres understood and immediately flew to Cairo, where he assured Moussa that he would do everything he could to force a change in the PLO meetings law. Moussa informed him that Arafat wanted to send the new Clinton administration a clear-cut message that the PLO was a partner in the peace negotiations. He demanded the ban on meeting the PLO be revoked immediately. On November 25, a Peres ally, Justice Minister David Libai, introduced into the cabinet a bill to rescind the law.

For the next month, Rabin joined the opposition in the fight against changing the law. Once again Beilin flew to Cairo to beg for a little more time and assure the PLO that the Peres faction would win the day.

By February the law was finally revoked, and MK Yael Dayan was sent to Tunis the very next day as an appeasement to Arafat. The PLO had influenced the results of the Israeli election and had reaped two of the three rewards promised them. All that remained was a return to a land-for-peace approach at the peace talks.

The relevant documentation has been passed into the hands of the Likud leadership. In the event of such a drastic change of policy at the negotiating table, they are prepared to expose the illegal—and possibly treasonous—secret diplomacy of Peres and Beilin.

As the months went by, the editors gathered more information on how the Labor Party had betrayed the Israeli people. A second report on the scandal appeared in the cover story of the October 1993 issue.

Behind Rabin's Back: The Peres / PLO Plot

The Labor Party's official chronology of events leading up to Israel's recognition of the PLO has the seeds planted after the party assumed power. According to the official scenario, Deputy Foreign Minister Yossi Beilin got the "Gaza-Jericho First" ball rolling at an academic conference. The idea was subsequently pursued for a year at a Norwegian university through the offices of Terje Roed Larsen, a social scientist who had been researching the Israeli-Palestinian conflict. However, an overview of the activities that led to the signing in Washington tells a radically different story.

In January 1990, former science minister and current president Ezer Weizman met with PLO officials in London, where the "Gaza-Jericho First" option was proposed. He returned to Israel and reported on his meetings to Labor Party head Shimon Peres, who was then a member of the National Unity Government.

Peres was enthusiastic about Wiezman's report and wanted to act on it, but knew Shamir would never countenance secret or any other kinds of talks with the PLO. He decided that the only way to exploit the opening was to bring down the coalition. He assigned Adi Tamir and Nimrod Novick, his aides, the task of keeping the PLO talks alive, while asking his deputy, Yossi Beilin, to join him in felling the government.

Step one in the plan was to force the Shas Party to leave the government. Peres, as finance minister, was well-placed to succeed. He had gathered indisputable proof of Interior Minister Arye Deri's embezzlements and bribe-taking. Beilin approached Deri with the findings and gave him a choice: quit the government or face the legal consequences. Deri chose to lead his Shas Party out of the coalition.

Next, a strong issue was needed as a pretext for a nonconfidence motion. This was supplied by U.S. Secretary of State James Baker in February 1990. He asked the Israeli government to support a plan which bore his name. One of the clauses implicitly put Jerusalem up for negotiation, a state of affairs both he and

Peres knew Shamir could never support.

Shas further shocked its supporters by supporting the Baker plan and only their pressure made the party renege after eighty-eight days and return to the Likud fold.

Labor was now in opposition and its leader Peres began planning a victory in the next national elections. Beginning in June 1991, he sent Beilin to Cairo four times to negotiate with the PLO. Beilin offered Kamal Said and Mahmoud Abbas, two Arafat aides, a deal: in return for the PLO shifting Arab-Israeli votes to Labor in the upcoming national elections, they would get recognition and something close to a state.

On January 17, James Baker arrived in Cairo and informed Egyptian president Hosni Mubarak that he would join in any effort to remove the Likud from power. The methods discussed were to pressure Shamir for a settlement freeze or face the consequences of cancelled loan guarantees or American recognition of the PLO. Two days later, Beilin was in Cairo plotting with PLO officials to bring down Shamir using Baker's strategy.

The loan guarantees proved crucial. Until the month before the national elections in June 1992, it was assumed that the 250,000 recent immigrant voters from the CIS would support the Likud. Traditionally, recent immigrants support the governing party, partly because it brought them to Israel and partly because they haven't the familiarity with the political system to make a knowledgeable choice.

However, the immigration process had been a miserable failure and the new arrivals were told the reason was because Shamir was unable to obtain $10 billion in loan guarantees from the American government. Thus, believing that only Labor could obtain the money to ease their lives, they shifted their votes en masse to Rabin. Between them and the Arab votes garnered by the PLO, Labor and its ally to the left, Meretz, just squeezed out a victory. However, combined they still did not have a Jewish majority in the Knesset and could turn to only one party to fill out their coalition—crime-ridden Shas.

While Beilin continued his deceit in Oslo and the government offered repeated denials of contacts between Peres' ministry and the PLO, the road to the agreement hit major obstacles.

In February 1993, Secretary of State Warren Christopher flew to Damascus with a plan to shut the PLO out of the peace talks. Arafat, apprised of the plan, flew from Amman to Khartoum where he sat in on two meetings with Hassan Atourbi, leader of the Sudanese Islamic Fundamentalist Movement. There, the plan to bomb the World Trade Center was hatched with Arafat's approval. This was the PLO's warning to the Clinton administration that it would not be neutralized, a message that almost scuttled Peres' secret talks.

By September, the final blow was on the way. After months spent defending his two Shas cabinet comrades, Rabin was ordered by the Israeli supreme court to fire Arye Deri and Rafael Pinchasi. The Labor government was on the verge of losing its Jewish majority and, subsequently, its mandate for negotiating an agreement with the PLO.

The PLO wanted more time to consider the final mutual recognition pact, but they were told that Labor's days were numbered. It was sign now or never. The PLO relented and both sides rushed into an agreement. Rabin did not even bring the historic treaty to the Knesset for a national debate for fear Shas would refuse to support it.

The week before the deal was signed in Jerusalem and Tunis, Arafat flew to Amman to meet with King Hussein and high ranking PLO officials. According to the media, the discussions centered on the PLO's supposed financial woes. Many analysts decided that this time Arafat was bankrupt and that the PLO buckled and accepted the agreement days later out of financial desperation; thus the many conditions within the agreement were hammered out in just a few days.

In actual fact, the meeting was to ratify three years of secret negotiations, mollify various factions of the PLO, and get Jordan's approval and promise of instant support. A day after the Washington ceremony, Jordan signed a separate Declaration of Principles for Peace with Israel. In reality, this agreement, far from being a spontaneous reaction, was at least three months in the making. In June, Foreign Minister Peres had blurted out the existence of the agreement, which Jordan immediately denied.

Three days before the Washington signing, Rabin ratified a decision made earlier, allowing 187 members of the Hamas leadership which had been deported to Lebanon to return home three months early. Though Rabin had stated that week that Hamas could scuttle the agreement with the PLO, he nevertheless strengthened the organization by placing its strategic leadership in the battlefront. In the northern Israeli town of Kiryat Shemona, hundreds of demonstrators pelted the bus-loads of deportees with rocks. However, the political establishment did not protest in a similar fashion. In effect, Rabin's decision increased the likelihood of violent chaos.

There is no doubt that Rabin's strings were pulled by Peres who, according to the original coalition agreement in June 1992, was to stay out of the peace talks. Peres disobeyed the edict and while Rabin became enmeshed in the Deri scandal, came to an agreement with the PLO. The return of the deportees may have been Rabin's contribution to the ultimate failure of the mutual recognition pact.

Rabin was not informed of the secret negotiations until the second week in August. At that point he was presented with a *fait accompli*. The PLO activists in the territories had already been starved into submission, and the Israeli public was to be manipulated into acceptance with pro-agreement rallies and favorable media reaction. All that was left for the prime minister was to lift a pen and sign.

Rabin had no choice. Powerful political forces were lined up against him. If he didn't sign he would face the wrath of the State Department, the European Community, moderate Arab states, his dovish Meretz coalition partner, and the majority of his own party.

November 1993

Israel's Secret Deal with Iran

Last July, in the aftermath of the week-long Israeli shelling of southern Lebanon, a cease-fire was agreed to in Damascus. Israel made a remarkable concession: it permitted Hizbollah attacks against its forces in the Israeli-controlled security zone in southern Lebanon. The agreement was part of a secret pact between Israel and Iran.

In the fall of 1992, Foreign Minister Shimon Peres, using the services of the French Foreign Office, brokered a deal with the Syrians which included the eventual relinquishment of the Golan Heights. The Rabin government immediately began a "Syria-first" policy which required convincing the Israeli public that the Golan Heights were not essential to its security, and that Syrian president Hafez el Assad was a serious peace partner.

The strategy failed and the public backlash persuaded the government that it would be forced to change the terms of its secret agreement with Syria. At this point the Foreign Ministry switched gears and initiated a "Palestine-first" strategy.

The Israelis asked the Iranians to strengthen their hand against the Syrians by manipulating Hizbollah into timely attacks against IDF and Southern Lebanese Army forces. In this way, Rabin could say that unless Syria restrained Hizbollah it was not entering into sincere peace negotiations.

After the Israel-PLO Recognition Pact was signed, Israel and the U.S. cut deals with Teheran to cease its support of terrorist organizations planning to sabotage the agreement. Amongst the Palestinian groups ordered to desist from anti-Israel attacks were those led by Nabil Hawatmeh, Ahmed Jabril, and George Habash.

At last month's Rejectionist Front meeting in Damascus, Iran sent Mahmoud Rafsanjani, brother of the Iranian president, with the following orders to the participants: talk up a good fight, but take no action.

Meanwhile the American government appointed former State Department official Richard Shifter, who served on the Israel desk, to negotiate an exchange with Iran: no torpedoing of the peace talks in return for the release of billions of dollars worth of assets frozen after the American Embassy in Teheran was overrun in 1979.

The Iranian government is nearing bankruptcy and is terrified of a popular uprising; hence its cooperation with Israel and the U.S. in assuring a relatively terrorism-free peace process, and pressuring Syria to accept permanent Israeli control over at least some of the Golan Heights.

California Schemin'

The Friday before the Israel-PLO accord was announced, Foreign Minister Peres flew to California for a secret meeting with Secretary of State Warren Christopher, returning to Israel the next day.

Peres feared transmitting his message by fax or phone from Jerusalem due to Rabin's intelligence monitoring of Peres' secret negotiations with the PLO since March.

What Peres told Christopher was that Rabin was hesitating and, despite severe pressure from the Americans for the previous several months, he was going to back out of recognizing the PLO. Rabin's intense distrust of Arab intentions was winning over the persuasion campaign.

Peres requested American help in pushing Rabin back into line. So far, Christopher's arguments to Rabin have not been revealed, but nonetheless, they were entirely persuasive. By Monday Rabin had fallen in line.

To force the American Jewish community to accept the Oslo deal, Labor realized that AIPAC had to be neutralized.

Labor's Plot Against AIPAC

Earlier this year, Harold Katz of Brooklyn taped a phone call with AIPAC official David Steiner in which Steiner claimed AIPAC was effectively determining President Clinton's upcoming cabinet. This was the first blow against the Likud-leaning leadership of the Jewish lobby. But it was not the last.

According to a reliable source within the Labor Party, one of the preliminary objectives of the process leading to recognition of the PLO was the elimination of AIPAC as a likely obstacle to American Jewish community acceptance of the planned agreement.

Six months before the Washington signing, Labor officials in the U.S. began plotting the downfall of the incumbent AIPAC leadership. Their tactics called for the removal of top AIPAC executives, with the help of high ranking Clinton aides tied to Peace Now.

Next to go was AIPAC president Tom Dine. The smear campaign against him was based on an obscure passage found in a book about Orthodox Jews by David Landau, a journalist whose Labor sympathies were established during his years at the *Jerusalem Post*. In a few lines, Landau quoted Dine as saying that Orthodox Jews smelled bad. Dine denies making the statement. However, these words landed in most of the editorial departments of the nation's newspapers and effectively ended Dine's career at AIPAC.

Next in line was Dine's deputy, Harvey Friedman, who, in a private conversation, called Deputy Foreign Minister Yossi Beilin "a little slimeball" in response to Beilin's alleged calls for the entire West Bank and Golan to be relinquished. The Israeli government protested the description and Friedman was forced to resign.

Dine's replacement, Steve Grossman, is an active leader of the Massachusetts Democratic Party and raised significant funds for President Clinton's election campaign.

Without the AIPAC of old, American Jews overwhelmingly accepted the Israel-PLO pact without any organized opposing voices. Until Steiner resigned, throughout AIPAC's long history no executive had been forced out of office by a scandal. Now within a few months of each other, three top AIPAC leaders had been felled by rumor and innuendo.

Getting Rid of Barak

In the past six months, the list of prominent figures who want IDF chief-of-staff Ehud Barak removed has grown dramatically. Among the personages who have expressed extreme dissatisfaction with Barak are president Ezer Weizman; Labor Party secretary Nissim Zvilli; cabinet ministers Yossi Sarid, Ora Namir, Binyamin Ben Eliezer, Shimon Sheetret, Haim Ramon, and Mordechai Gur; Defense Ministry director-general David Ivri; former president Chaim Herzog, and opposition MKs Raful Eitan and Yitzhak Shamir.

The government critics maintain that Barak is more interested in politics than security and that the IDF is suffering. Most of the critics complain that Rabin is going to grant Barak's wish by naming him defense minister, but Ora Namir goes a step further saying, "He's aiming for prime minister and he doesn't care if it's under Labor or Likud."

Eitan and Shamir's complaints are that Barak is incompetent and that during his tenure the IDF has suffered needlessly from fatal accidents; poor battlefield performance, especially against Hizbollah; and a noticeable drop in morale and quality.

Former military liaison officer to Washington, General Uzi Lev-Tsur, doesn't understand why Rabin appointed Barak chief-of-staff in the first place.

"The failure of the Lebanon War was the inability of the central force to complete its mission," he says. "The eastern and coastal forces attained their goals in days but the division led by Barak and former commander of Judea and Samaria, Amiram Mitzneh failed. Yet these are the officers Rabin chose to lead the IDF in putting down the intifada. I'm very worried how the IDF will perform in the next war if it's led by Barak."

Other critics of Barak hint that he is covering up his role in last year's Tzeelim tragedy in which five soldiers died in a training accident. Barak was the highest ranking officer present at the operation, yet he has not been implicated in the investigation. For that matter, no high ranking officer has been charged with negligence.

Rabin is unconcerned about the criticism. In fact, he is encouraging Barak's political dreams. He recently chose Barak over a qualified cabinet minister to represent him in a meeting with American Vice-President Al Gore.

However, Barak was left out of the PLO recognition negotiations and showed his immediate displeasure by publicly criticizing the lack of security considerations in the agreement. Rabin took the hint and when Secretary of State Warren Christopher visited Israel to discuss the PLO recognition pact, the prime minister invited only Peres and Barak to a closed door meeting.

It was Peres, as defense minister in 1976, who appointed Barak chief of the Northern Command, and Rabin who handed him the office of chief-of-staff in which the consensus is that he has performed miserably. Nonetheless, Rabin will not remove him— no matter how many setbacks, accidents, and cover-ups occur in the IDF.

In fact, Rabin wants to extend Barak's tenure for another year. After that the Defense Ministry might be his.

December 1993

> *At the time,* Inside Israel *readers thought the editors had gone too far in accusing the government of planning to divide Jerusalem. The common reaction was that as suicidal as this government was, even*

it would not divide Jerusalem.

Further, Teddy Kollek, after over a quarter of a century of declaring Jerusalem would never be divided, could not be so two-faced as to be behind the scheme.

In July 1996 Oslo negotiator Yair Hirschfeld let the cat out of the bag. In interviews to Israel Radio and Nativ magazine he divulged the plans for Jerusalem concocted by Kollek and Yossi Beilin. Beilin denied Hirschfeld's version of events for several days before confirming it in a TV interview.

Inside Israel was on target back in December of 1993. The Rabin government was searching for a formula to redivide Israel's capital and Teddy Kollek was the main mover behind the plot.

Planning Jerusalem's Future

For the past six months, the government has been taking advice on the future of Jerusalem from a planning commission whose members include Sophie Eldar, chairperson of the Ministry of Housing's building committee; Nira Sidi, a manager at the Israel Land Authorities Office; Amos Marmon, an executive at the Interior Ministry; Uzi Wexler, director-general of the Jerusalem Development Corporation and a close aide of Teddy Kollek; and Raanan Weitz, formerly the settlement director of the Jewish Agency.

The forum is not merely an academic exercise. It is preparing plans to be presented to the PLO in negotiations.

At a secret meeting on September 9, one day before Prime Minister Rabin signed the recognition agreement with the PLO in Israel, the forum met secretly and approved in principle a plan for Jerusalem concocted by Weitz, which he calls Metropolitan Jerusalem.

The plan calls for the building of a new wing of Jerusalem called El Kuds that will house 300,000 Palestinian refugees. The new development will be situated next to the large Jewish neighborhood of Pisgat Zeev and will effectively cut off another Jewish neighborhood, Neve Yaacov, from the rest of the city. All 80,000 Jews will be isolated by El Kuds. The forum's plan is for those Israeli citizens to live under Palestinian authority.

Jerusalem itself will be divided, though nominally it will remain one city with a permanent Jewish mayor and Arab deputy. The Lebanization of the city continues, with plans to restrict Arab development to the area east toward the Dead Sea and Jewish development to the west in the direction of Bet Shemesh. As for the Old City, it will be divided into municipal districts, each run separately by Jews, Moslems, and Christians.

The plan, which implicitly recognizes a Palestinian state with Jerusalem as its capital and specifically promotes the division of the city, runs counter to every statement about the future of Jerusalem made by the current government. However, one voice has unexpectedly come out in support of one part of it. King Hussein of Jordan believes the Old City is too important to be left in the hands of the PLO. He prefers that a council of the world's major religions oversee the district. Included in the council would be Shiites from Iran.

Chapter Three

January 1994

While the mainstream press neglected Foreign Minister Peres' secret ties to various French politicians, Inside Israel realized very early on that Israel's foreign policy was being pulled toward the Europeans by Peres and toward the Americans by Rabin. The January 1994 issue reported on two foreign policy agendas by Peres—both in direct opposition to Rabin's wishes and conducted behind his back.

Peres' French Connection

Foreign Minister Shimon Peres has been rigorously pursuing Prime Minister Rabin and his intelligence allies through the French foreign minister, Alain Juppe.

In late October Peres informed the French that the Mossad had placed an agent close to PLO chief Yasser Arafat. The information was duly transferred to the Tunisian police who arrested the spy. The accused was deputy head of PLO internal security, Adnan Yassin. Yassin's car was discovered to be rigged with state-of-the-art communications equipment and was packed with Semtex explosives. They were thought to have been planted for use against Arafat in the event that Israel was forced to back out of the agreement it had signed with him.

As fantastic as the story appears, Yassin confessed to the plot. Peres' leak was reported by newspapers as diverse as Jordan's *Al Dustor*, *Al Hayat* of Saudi Arabia, and *Yerushalayim* in Israel. According to these publications, Peres informed a PLO signatory of the agreement with Israel, Mahmoud Abbas, who passed the information to the French.

Abbas has long-standing ties with Peres. In 1991 he and Peres reached an agreement in Cairo that if the PLO recruited Arab-Israeli voters for Labor in the June 1992 election, the organization would be rewarded with recognition and autonomy after Labor won.

On November 12, 1993, while Prime Minister Rabin was in Washington, Peres was recorded speaking to Juppe about reopening the Syrian peace front under French auspices. The year before, Peres and the French had pushed a "Syria-first" policy on Rabin which backfired when most Israelis polled adamantly refused to give up the Golan Heights.

The Americans want no French interference in the Middle East and decided to work with Rabin on torpedoing Peres' program. With Secretary of State Warren Christopher's approval, Rabin ordered an air attack on Hizbollah positions in the Syrian-controlled Bekaa Valley of Lebanon. This was the first such attack since the signing of the recognition pact with the PLO, in large part because Peres was opposed to such tactics.

Though Rabin told Washington-based journalists that the air strike was in retaliation for Hizbollah attacks on Israeli positions in southern Lebanon, in fact it was a strong message to Peres and the Syrians that the defense minister has more authority than the over-independent foreign minister.

Peres Signs Secret Deal with Jordan

Without fanfare last November, Foreign Minister Shimon Peres initialled an actual peace treaty with Jordan. The foreign minister secretly drove to Amman via Aqaba, where he was received in a manner usually reserved for visiting royalty. After a grueling nine-hour session he battered out a treaty, which to his delight was initialled by Crown Prince Hassan.

Among the terms of the peace with Jordan, Israel promised to accept Jordanian sovereignty over disputed lands near the Dead Sea, which Jordan would lease in perpetuity to Israel for a nominal fee. Peres also committed Israel to intervene militarily if the Hashemite kingdom was ever attacked by a third party; Jordan did not make the same commitment to Israel. Another clause in the treaty commits Israel to use its influence in Congress to have Jordanian debts to the U.S. forgiven.

To get the treaty off to a good start, President Clinton committed himself to personally chair a Middle East economic conference in Amman, and to press for international financial backing for Israeli-Jordanian development projects.

No sooner had Peres flown back to Jerusalem than leaks from him and Police Minister Moshe Shachal appeared in the Israeli media promising a peace treaty with Jordan "within weeks."

However, the moment Peres left the Hashemite court, King Hussein phoned Syrian president Hafez el Assad to inform him of the visit. Assad was not amused by what he heard and a message was broadcast shortly after on Damascus radio warning Hussein that a separate peace with Israel would lead "to internal difficulties within Jordan." Translated into the parlance of the Middle East, Assad was threatening Hussein's life if he made peace before Syria.

Seemingly unaware of regional realities, Peres remained convinced that he had personally arranged a peace treaty with Jordan that King Hussein would quickly acknowledge. It took the idealistic foreign minister a few weeks to fall off his cloud and stop the media leaks that peace with Jordan was at hand.

February 1994

In February 1994, Inside Israel *chose as its lead story the actual chain of events that forced President Clinton to meet Syrian president Hafez el Assad in Geneva. While itself eye-opening, it was the second story of the issue that introduced—for the first time on its pages— another major player in the New World Order games being played over Jerusalem: the Vatican.*

The Assad / Clinton Geneva Understanding

The main purpose of the Geneva meeting between President Clinton of America and President Assad of Syria was to strengthen Syria's role in the peace process and to diminish, if not eliminate, the PLO's role.

Syria, for several reasons, is deeply opposed to the Principles of Understanding signed by Israel and the PLO on September 13. The first is that the leadership of the Arab world shifted dramatically to the Egyptian/PLO axis, or the so-called moderates. Syria and her allies suddenly found themselves left out of the mainstream of Middle East diplomacy and feared they would not benefit from its potential rewards. Assad deeply dislikes Arafat and found his reappearance on center stage both galling and threatening.

In October the Syrians threatened to abandon the Washington peace talks altogether in protest of President Clinton's backing of an agreement between Israel and the PLO before Syria, and his perceived favoritism of the Mubarak/Arafat diplomatic direction.

The Americans originally took the attitude that Syria would eventually fall in line, but by early November had decided that not only was Assad not budging from his original stance, but that the Israel/PLO talks were going nowhere and would most likely fail. At some point in the first week of November, Clinton decided that no real peace could be achieved without the Syrians. He ordered the State Department to explore the possibility of reopening the Syrian channel.

On November 12 Prime Minister Rabin rushed to Washington, reportedly on a mission to receive increased American aid. Less reported was that he was accompanied by former defense minister Ariel Sharon. In 1974, during his first tenure as prime minister, Rabin had appointed Sharon his advisor on security matters. Sharon resigned the post in protest over the Rabin/Kissinger secret diplomacy with Syria concerning the future of Lebanon. At that time Syria agreed not to raise a fuss over the continued Israeli presence on the Golan Heights in return for Israeli noninterference in Syrian/Lebanese affairs. In 1976, Syria attacked Lebanon and turned it into a puppet state.

Nonetheless, Rabin did not cut his private ties with Sharon. Though he insisted that Sharon's presence was coincidental, in fact Sharon was sent to the Pentagon to explain the opposition of the Israeli security establishment to the ongoing American/Syrian secret talks.

The trip failed, and by December 6 Secretary of State Warren Christopher was in Damascus for a meeting between Syrian vice-president Hassan Habibi and Jordanian Hamas leader Ibrahim Rusha.

The goals of the Syrians were spelled out clearly for Christopher. They wanted free elections in the Administered Territories, which Hamas had every reason to believe it would win. The final result of such a victory would be the end of the PLO's role as the preeminent player in the peace process with Israel and the demise of Yasser Arafat.

In return for ousting the PLO from the peace process, Syria agreed to disband the rejectionist front—including Hizbollah—and turn it into a strictly political movement. Simply, Syria agreed to stop sponsoring terrorism.

The Syrians also wanted a summit between Assad and Clinton, which would symbolize an American change of diplomatic direction. Christopher informed the Syrians this would be impossible unless Assad publicly announced his intention of reaching a peace accord with Israel. Once Assad acquiesced, the Geneva meeting was on.

None of the proceedings were lost on Arafat. Prior to the summit, Arafat appealed desperately to both Assad and Clinton to allow him to participate at Geneva. He was flatly rejected. He attempted to go to Geneva privately, in a feeble attempt to steal the show from the two presidents and to preserve his position by exposing the purpose of the meeting. The Swiss turned down his visa application and told him, "Wait your turn."

Rabin was no happier at this turn of events. Prior to the Geneva meeting he planned his answer. If the Americans insisted on the Syrian line, he would let the Israeli people decide events in a national referendum.

The Americans responded to the referendum announcement coolly. They know that Syria—with its ally Hamas—is now the strongest potential partner in any peace talks with Israel and that the PLO road is nonviable. The Geneva meeting was, then, the first step in changing the direction of the peace trail toward Damascus.

While the Israeli media generally lauded the Vatican's decision to establish diplomatic relations with Israel, the editors of Inside Israel *understood that Deputy Foreign Minister Yossi Beilin was doing the Vatican's bidding. The pope wanted holy real estate in Jerusalem before the apocalyptic year 2000, and* Inside Israel *uncovered solid evidence that Beilin had made just such an arrangement with the Holy See.*

Israel's relationship with the Vatican took on a completely new look during the Rabin-Peres administration. Half a year after this story was published, Inside Israel *investigated the agreement signed between Israel and the Vatican, and found it contained a number of secret clauses which were never reported to the Knesset or the public.*

Beilin's Vatican Sell-Out

The price Israel paid for recent diplomatic recognition by the Vatican is another example of Deputy Foreign Minister Yossi Beilin's self-serving program. The Vatican has not moved from its position of distrust of Israel or Jews. It must be recalled that since his investiture the current pope, John Paul II, has pursued a pro-Arab diplomatic policy which came to full blossom in the days preceding the Persian Gulf War when the Vatican evinced unseemly sympathy with the goals of Iraqi president Saddam Hussein. During John Paul's tenure, a nunnery was erected on the site of the Auschwitz death camp in his native Poland, creating a major rift with world Jewry.

The Vatican made no attempts to establish any sort of dialogue with Israel until the Madrid Middle East Peace Conference in October of 1991. At that point, the Holy See approved a permanent council to resolve differences with Israel. The motivation for the decision was mostly fear. The Vatican maintains a significant number of churches and institutions in the Administered Territories. For instance, its library inside the Church of the Nativity in Bethlehem is invaluable. With the growing possibility of a change in the status quo, the Catholic church in Rome did not want to be left out of negotiations affecting its property.

By July of 1993 discussions had reached Foreign Ministry level, but no breakthroughs were in sight. Israel's signing of the Declaration of Principles with the PLO in September 1993, changed the pace of papal negotiations with Israel. Previously, the Vatican had assumed that its properties would remain under Israeli control for an indefinite period. Suddenly, it was confronted with the prospect of its treasures falling into the hands of the PLO.

Yitzhak Rabin with Pope John Paul II, 1994

There was panic in the Holy See, and in November Beilin chose to exploit the opportunity and personally took over negotiations with the Vatican. He smelled a diplomatic coup that could only enhance his reputation and went to work. The Vatican had one objective, while Beilin had many. The pope wanted the church's properties protected and ordered his chief negotiator, Monsignor Claudio Chile, to arrange extraterritorial status for them as a way of keeping them from falling into the hands of the PLO in the future.

Beilin had several demands of his own. He wanted full diplomatic recognition, including an exchange of ambassadors. Among his other demands was that priceless Jewish historical books in the Vatican library be transferred to Israel.

The Vatican's negotiator quickly detected how desperate Beilin was for some form of diplomatic recognition. In exchange for such an agreement, the Vatican wanted the right to build on Mount Zion in Jerusalem, and to receive tax exemptions for this and all other church properties in Israel.

Beilin agreed to the two demands, which were included in a separate, secret accord. As for the treasury of Jewish literature, the best the Vatican would offer was open access to its archives. In return for giving in to all the Vatican's wishes, the pope signed a recognition accord with Israel, missing one vital clause: an exchange of ambassadors. After the accord was signed, the Foreign Ministry attempted to appoint Rabbi David Rosen as its ambassador to the Vatican, but the Holy See would not approve the move (purportedly because a rabbi was deemed inappropriate to the position).

Not everyone at the Foreign Ministry approved of the manner in which Beilin had sold Israel so cheaply. The ministry's legal affairs spokeswoman, Esther Samilag, complained about the various capitulations and was subsequently transferred to the Israeli embassy in Katmandu, Nepal.

Other Foreign Ministry employees, more discreet in their opposition to the Vatican agreement, have merely leaked details of

it. MK Avraham Shapira was one recipient of the leaked information, and he publicly demanded to know if Israel has exempted
the Vatican from property taxes and given away building permits
on Mount Zion. Deputy mayor of Jerusalem Shmuel Meir went
one step further; he claimed he had received "information that
properties promised to the Vatican in Jerusalem would be granted
extraterritorial status." He also demanded that Beilin publish the
full text of the pact.

The response from Beilin's office is revealing. It does not deny
the secret clauses, but rather admits, "Included in the Vatican agreement is the issue of papal properties in Israel that will be resolved
by a committee of experts that has already been formed."

If such a committee is in existence, its work is not being publicized. What is gradually being revealed by perturbed aides and
Foreign Ministry workers is the tale of an obsessed politician once
again putting his own interests ahead of the country's.

March 1994

In January Barry Chamish answered his phone and received a
remarkable offer. The caller insisted that he had acquired highly
classified documents secreted out of Yossi Beilin's office in the Foreign
Ministry, and that he was acting as an interlocutor for someone
working inside the office. The "someone" was appalled by the cables
he had read from Oslo and elsewhere, and had cautiously copied
them. They were released to the Jerusalem Post and were used as
the basis for a front-page article exposing the government's real policy
of pushing Israel back to the 1967 borders.

This was one of the few times that the superficial
Jerusalem Post conducted a genuine investigation of
government conduct or any other sensitive subject. In
retaliation, the Foreign Ministry cancelled 1,300
subscriptions, costing the paper over $40,000.

Chamish met the interlocutor in the lobby of a Jerusalem hotel, *where he was handed a long computer printout. After a cursory glance he realized he was holding explosive material. This, he was told, was the stuff the Post wouldn't print. Inside Israel had established a name for courage and might be the only publication that would dare to make the document public.*

Courageous perhaps, but suicidal, no. Chamish called Steve Rodan, the reporter who used the document as the basis for the now infamous Jerusalem Post story. He said, "The document checks out and so does the author. We checked and rechecked both of them for three months and received confirmation of the facts right up to the cabinet level."

The editorial board of the stodgy Post (out of fear of even worse government reprisals) nixed the information that Inside Israel chose to publish. One claim was too much—by far—for the editors of Inside Israel to take responsibility for. The document claimed that Beilin's plan for emptying the territories of Jewish residents included instilling panic by having local settler leaders killed. However, there was circumstantial evidence to back this seemingly preposterous assertion, and the editors chose to present it with the headline, "Are the Settlers Paranoid?"

Of all the material the editors gathered, this was the most frightening for the country, and for themselves personally.

The Hidden Clauses of Oslo

One senior Foreign Ministry official has documented the Israel-PLO negotiations and, through a second party, has permitted them to be leaked to the Israeli media.

The shocking indictment of Deputy Foreign Minister Yossi Beilin could be dismissed, unless some factors are taken into account. The official was a member of Beilin's "Peace Team" and was privy to the most highly-classified Foreign Ministry documents. As a ranking diplomatic aide, he was a firsthand witness to the origins and development of the secret Oslo negotiations.
The PISGA

The Foreign Ministry program for Israel's future is outlined in a document authored by Beilin himself called *The Palestine Interim Self-Government Agreement* (PISGA). When first prepared, the document was classified by the Foreign Ministry as a proposal submitted by the joint Jordanian-Palestinian delegation to the Washington talks, in order to obfuscate its authorship and true policy significance.

The PISGA has been incorporated into other local media reports about deception in the peace process. The main points are that the ultimate aims of the peace process are to roll back Israel's territory to the 1949 borders; to create a Palestinian "entity" which, after an interim period, will be granted statehood; to accede to this state exclusive rights to underground water resources geologically shared by both states; and to permit the right of return for any Palestinian to the new nation.

The PISGA purportedly describes a plan to disarm settlers and force them to evacuate the West Bank and Gaza Strip, after which no Jews will be permitted to reside in the areas. Parts of this plan may have already been put into force.

Illegitimacy . . .

Beilin is said to have personally authored or authorized another policy paper, revealingly titled *The Illegitimacy of Israeli Sovereignty Over Jerusalem*. It outlines the government's program for the future of Jerusalem. (See *Inside Israel*, Dec. 1993.) By calling for the division of the Old City into cantons whose border posts will be under U.N. control, Israelis will be barred from freely entering East Jerusalem, while access to West Jerusalem will be severely restricted for Arabs. In effect, Jerusalem will once again become a divided city.

Israel Started the Six-Day War

One of Beilin's greatest worries was that a future Likud government would short-circuit his plan for a Palestinian state during the interim period by resettling the remaining lands outside Jericho and the Gaza Strip. To counter such a possibility, the program calls for Israel to pass a law declaring itself the aggressor in the Six-Day War. To justify such a misreading of history, Beilin cited such legal texts as *Palestine and International Law* by Henry Cattan and Gerard von Glahn's *Law Among Nations,* which stress the illegality of Israel's presence in the Administered Territories. The ration-alization for the declaration of aggression is that if Israel took the disputed territories illegally, it would have no right under international law in the future to settle or retrieve them.

American Cooperation
The ongoing negotiations between Israel and the PLO are largely theatrics. The peace program has already been written by Beilin, Shimon Peres, and the PLO's Abu Mazin. It was submitted for Washington's approval in September 1993, was upgraded in November, and formally (though covertly) authorized by Secretary of State Warren Christopher during his visit to Jerusalem in December.

The Americans promised to solve intractable problems; i.e. water. Beilin gave away to the PLO the underground reservoir that supplies 30 percent of Israel's water needs. To compensate for the loss, America offered to build Israel two large desalinization plants.

This solution did nothing to salve the anger of Israeli hydrologists, who observed that desalinized water could not be produced in the quantities needed to run industry and agriculture and will increase the cost of drinking water beyond the consumers' ability to pay.

Keeping Shas in Line
Beilin was well aware of the flimsy nature of his government's coalition as he prepared his program. He realized that if the Shas Party refused to support his plans, then they would fail. Since the constituency of Shas is largely opposed to closer—or any—ties with the PLO, a party decision to oppose Labor's legislation was viewed as a likelihood, unless steps were taken to keep members

in line. The method of ensuring control was organized blackmail.

After an extensive investigation, with the cooperation of the U.S. Justice Department and the FBI, Israeli government investigators managed to trace some $600,000 of Shas leader Arye Deri's embezzled funds to drug money-laundering operations in the U.S. and Belgium. The Justice Ministry and the Police Ministry kept these crimes out of Deri's indictments.

In the event that Shas chooses to throw Deri to the legal dogs some day, the Justice Department has prepared indictments against the sons of party spiritual leader Rabbi Ovadia Yosef. Strong cases have been prepared against each of them for embezzlement in the $50–100,000 range.

At the time it was concocted, the thorn in the Shas blackmail strategy was Attorney-General Yosef Harish. He was replaced in the late fall of 1993 with a more compliant politico, Micha Ben Yair. Since taking up his new post, Ben Yair has covered up the crimes of Shas. He has been holding them in escrow until the day that Shas threatens to stop supporting the current peace process.

The Campaign Against the Settlers and Their Supporters

The Beilin plan calls for the removal of all Jews from beyond the Green Line. Before such a change can be implemented, opposition from the settlers of the Administered Territories is to be eliminated. Beilin is well aware that tens of thousands of Jewish territorial residents will fight his program and that they will have broad support throughout the country; thus, if they are to be removed, he has decided it will have to be in stages.

Stage one calls for the disarming of the settlers, and the process has already begun in earnest. Since last December hundreds of guns have been confiscated from settlers, while notifications of license cancellations have been sent to many others.

Once the settlers become less able to defend themselves, army presence on the roads leading to their homes will be greatly diminished, leading to heavy terrorist casualties along with feelings of fear and helplessness. This will cause the more passive residents to panic, sell their homes, and flee. With the resulting crash in housing prices, the government will offer to buy up the homes of all other settlers wishing to move, at current market value; thus, the settlers can be evacuated without paying the high cost incurred when the government gave up the Sinai in 1979.

Kafka Visits Hebron

Clearly, thousands of residents committed to staying in their homes will see through the plan and resist it. Beilin's program calls for instilling increased fear in the rebels. This will require a great deal of intelligence material to counteract their resistance.

To facilitate this need, Beilin requested and received a significant expansion of army intelligence (Aman), in order to supply the general security services (Shabak) with information required for total suppression of opposition voices.

New surveillance equipment installed at Beilin's suggestion monitors all international phone and fax communications. The equipment is programmed to do real-time scanning for key words which, when spoken or written, automatically switch on recording equipment. On a more personal level, the entire phone system of Hebron has been tapped, while hundreds of individuals living elsewhere are being listened to.

Aman has expanded its database of potential opposition activists to include detailed cross-checks, while the Shabak has infiltrated the settlements with dozens of spies.

Dehumanizing the Settlers

In order to take his program to its extremes, Beilin had to take precautions so that violence against settlers would not provoke a sympathetic reaction from other Israelis, which would be translated into opposition to the peace process as he created it.

Dehumanizing the settlers required, first, delegitimizing them. This was to be accomplished with a media campaign aimed at painting the residents of the territories as fanatics. Once such an image had been planted, the settlers would no longer be identified by most Israelis as one of them. It would then be easier to have a small number killed to break the morale of the rest.

To finance an expensive state-of-the-art public relations campaign Beilin turned to Peres, who solicited the necessary start-up funds, some $6.5 million, from French millionaire and close friend Jean Friedman.

A Few Extraditions for the Cause

Beilin's plan calls for the government to consider drafting a law which will permit the extradition of Jews to Palestine for crimes against Palestinians. There, they will be subject to Palestinian criminal law. Beilin believes that Jewish retaliatory actions will be stopped cold if the perpetrators are sent to the Palestinian entity for trial and possible execution.

Are the Settlers Paranoid?

Many settlers and their supporters believe they are the victims of a planned program of executions. Some contend that their government was behind an initiative to destroy the settler movement by eliminating its most determined proponents. Their fear was fueled by the coincidental nature of terrorist attacks just previous to the massacre.

In the first attack in Kiryat Arba, two members of the Lapid family, a father and son, were shot dead in their van by passing gunmen. His widow, Miriam, is number four on the right-wing Moledet Party list. The next attack was a failed attempt on the life of David Axelrod, spokesman for the Kahane Chai movement. The third attack was an ambush on the former member of the Knesset for the opposition National Religious Party, Haim Druckman.

With so many potential victims, the advocates of the execution theory contend the attacks had to have been orchestrated.

News of the robberies at Prof. Uri Millstein's home and office

convinced the editors that this was a man they had to meet. Millstein
was most verbose about the cover-up of Rabin's incompetent military
career but refused to believe that perhaps Rabin's very incompetence
was being directed by forces in America and London.

However, after some thought Millstein did impart information
that backed the editors' thesis. He said that in 1977 Jimmy Carter
forced Menachem Begin to appoint Moshe Dayan his foreign minister.
Dayan, whose deliberate inaction led to the debacle of the Yom Kippur
War was considered finished in politics, but was ordered revived by
Carter's advisers in the State Department. Later, it was Dayan who
persuaded Begin to accept far-reaching concessions at Camp David,
Maryland.

Rabin's Robbers

On two occasions in January, intruders attempted to steal the files
on Yitzhak Rabin collected by historian Dr. Uri Millstein. The first
attempt to break into his home failed when the criminals were
detected. The second attempt a day later at Millstein's office was
more successful. Although they did not abscond with any documents, the intruders were able to destroy a significant amount of
material Dr. Millstein calls "essential" before their mission was
interrupted unexpectedly by his assistant, Ariella Yakir.

Millstein and Yakir filed police complaints, not just for the
break-in but for suspected illegal surveillance "by the Shabak and
other security agencies."

The book Millstein is currently writing is called *The Rabin File*.
If it is anything like his previous work, *A History of the Israeli War
of Independence*, then the prime minister has cause for concern.
Millstein claimed that Rabin was "a major example of a military
commander whose failures, by mutual agreement within the elite,
were swept under the rug. . . . He failed more than any other
commander in 1948 in each of his posts."

Among Rabin's failures reported in the book is his conduct as
the head of operations of the Palmach Infantry Brigade. As the

officer responsible for keeping the Tel Aviv-Jerusalem corridor open, he was utterly unsuccessful. The road was never secured and hundreds died in ambushes. On March 24, 1948, Rabin was stripped of his command but mysteriously, three weeks later, was appointed commander of the Harel Brigade.

On April 20, Rabin ran from the battlefield, leaving his soldiers trapped under Arab fire. Three days later, while dozens of Harel fighters were dying in the battle at Nebi Samuel, Rabin was nowhere to be found. David Ben Gurion personally sought him out and found him asleep at army headquarters. On May 17, Rabin was ousted from his post at the insistence of the army high command.

As chief-of-staff of the IDF in 1967, Rabin suffered a nervous collapse two weeks before the outbreak of the Six-Day War and threatened to surrender before a shot was fired. When the war broke out, Rabin disappeared for the first few days. There was speculation that he had suffered another nervous breakdown, though his friends denied this, claiming he was "only drunk."

Dr. Millstein claims these events are the tip of the iceberg, and his new work on Rabin will present the whole story . . . if it is ever published in anything like the form in which it is currently being written. Today's minister of defense, Yitzhak Rabin, will likely demand that the IDF censorship office take a long, hard look at the book, as it did two years ago when author Mati Golan's revelations about the Kissinger/Rabin secret diplomacy following the Yom Kippur War were censored and publication of the work was delayed for eight months.

Chapter Four

May 1994

> *While few other journalists realized how important the issue was, the editors wrote about the growing discontent in the IDF over Rabin's peace deal.*

IDF Officers Rebel

Dozens of IDF officers signed a protest advertisement that appeared in Israeli newspapers in March. The highest ranking signatory was Res. General Yermi Olmert.

The public notice read, "The surrender to terror is the only achievement of the negotiations with the PLO, which threaten our survival. Shaking hands with terrorists means terror has won. Arafat represents his own interests and will never fight for the security of Israel."

The IDF is experiencing a wave of defections. Among the officers who have opposed the current peace process are Ron Shenkar, deputy commander of the Hebron Reserve Brigade; military prosecutor Shimon Bart; and Captain Khagi Ben Artsi.

Shenkar has announced publicly that if ordered to evacuate settlements, he will refuse the command. This seriously complicates any government plan to remove Jewish residents from Hebron.

Bart has refused to do his reserve duty as a military prosecutor stating as his reason, "No matter how serious the crime, the IDF is letting PLO criminals off. They are no longer using legal standards to try terrorists, but political ones. I can't participate in courts that mete out public service sentences to firebombers."

Ben Artsi refuses to do reserve duty until the government agrees to a national referendum on the peace process. His claim to fame is being Likud leader Binyamin Netanyahu's brother-in-law. Netanyahu does not advocate refusal of service as a protest, and Ben Artsi's stand has driven a wedge between them.

Nonetheless, with so many IDF officers openly refusing to follow orders, the government will have a problem keeping a tight lid on what appears to be spreading mutiny among its military commanders.

During the early part of 1994 a meeting was arranged with Mordechai Nesiyahu, who left the editors with a revisionist history of the Oslo negotiations. His version of events was later confirmed in an interview with negotiator Ron Pundak.

Peres Fibs About Oslo

This year's biggest literary controversy so far centers around the exclusion of Deputy Foreign Minister Yossi Beilin from his boss Shimon Peres' book about the reconciliation with the PLO, and the exclusion of Peres from Beilin's book on the same subject.

According to Mordechai Nesiyahu, programming director of Beit Beryl, the Labor Party publishing house, Beilin did not leave Peres out for any personal reason, but rather because Peres was not involved at any level in the Oslo peace talks.

Nesiyahu's version of events is very different from any other so far made public. He insists that the genesis of the Oslo talks began in early November of 1992 when a left-wing academic, Yair Hirschfeld, met Abu Alah in a London hotel room. By a fateful and unbelievable coincidence, Hirschfeld left his meeting and ran into Yossi Beilin in the lobby of the hotel and reported that Abu Alah's attitude had changed and that the PLO were prepared to cut a deal.

Beilin noted the details of the meeting and reported them not to Shimon Peres, his superior, but directly to Prime Minister Rabin.

Beilin told Rabin that he had contacts in Norway who would agree to host secret talks between Israel and the PLO if Rabin would agree to authorize them. He added that he was prepared to continue working behind Peres' back at Rabin's behest.

Nesiyahu claims that Rabin studied a memo from him, recommending direct talks with Arafat based on his understanding that no agreement with the Palestinians was possible without the cooperation of the PLO in Tunis. Because of Nesiyahu's obvious desire to be credited with a role in the Oslo talks, Labor Party supporters of Shimon Peres have accused him of fomenting lies.

The Peres faction has good reason to worry. Nesiyahu intends to release his version of the peace process in a booklet published by Beit Beryl. Peres appealed to Rabin to intervene to stop publication of the Nesiyahu booklet, which Rabin refused. When Nesiyahu's report is released, Peres may have a lot of explaining to do.

According to Nesiyahu, for the first three months of the Oslo negotiations Peres was unaware of them. The only Israelis originally privy to the talks were Rabin, Beilin, Hirschfeld, and Pundak. In March 1993 attorney Yoel Zinger and Foreign Ministry director-general Uri Savir were let in on the secret. In late March when information about the talks finally reached Peres, he totally missed its significance and asked for no role in Oslo. Yet when the negotiations bore fruit, Peres took credit for being the driving force behind them.

Nesiyahu says, "Peres' book is a lie and when his true role in the negotiations is understood—that is, no role at all—he will be forced to resign as foreign minister."

If Nesiyahu's book is correct, Rabin will have some explaining to do. The prime minister maintained a public position of opposition to the dovish statements and acts of his party. In February he declared himself opposed to a change in the law banning meetings between the PLO and Israelis. At the same time as he was opposing such meetings in public, he was conducting secret negotiations that were against the law at the time.

Nesiyahu does not see that as a problem. He insists that Israeli law permits the prime minister to conduct secret diplomacy and if such talks are to succeed, he may be required to deceive the electorate and its representatives in the Knesset.

Nesiyahu applauds Rabin for his skillful use of disinformation aimed at promulgating a falsified history of the negotiations and of obfuscating his early role in them. His target is Peres for rewriting history by fraudulently placing himself in the center of it.

June 1994 was the first time Inside Israel *spoke about "Masonic manipulation" of the peace process. In May two newspapers,* Shishi *and* Yediot Achronot, *published pieces documenting Rabin's ties to the secret society. They could not be ignored.*

Brothers in Robes

Prime Minister Yitzhak Rabin and Jordanian King Hussein have more in common than that they are both Middle East leaders. Both are members of the Freemasons.

Hussein is open about his association with the Masons and has achieved a high degree of standing in the organization. He flies several times a year to attend Masonic functions in London.

Rabin is much more coy about his Masonic ties. A response from the prime minister's office on his ties to Masonry reads: "After Mr. Rabin completed his army career and just before becoming the ambassador to Washington, he was inducted into the Freemason movement. That was twenty-six years ago and since then, he has maintained no further ties to Masonry."

Rabin's denial is belied by a film of him presiding over a Masonic celebration in Jerusalem in 1976. Jerusalem is uniquely important to Masons since they trace their origins to the masons who built Solomon's Temple.

Though one is a proud member and the other coy about his

membership, it is not known if Rabin and Hussein view the future of Jerusalem in shared Masonic terms.

_____

By the spring of 1994 the editors also began to realize that one of Yossi Beilin's duties was to meld the IDF into a world army. He approached the task with vigor, sending Israeli troops to trouble spots far from the Middle East.

Getting More Involved in Angola

Four Israeli security experts, including Reserve General Yosef Bar On, were expelled from Angola in March. Bar On was the owner of a Luanda-based security firm, Ango-Sego, which was involved in guarding the country's oil installations against terrorism and training elite forces fighting the rebel UNITA movement.

According to the Angolan Foreign Ministry, Bar On used his armed men to stage a number of major heists against the country's diamond industry. Despite the expulsions, Angola wishes to continue its military ties with Israel, which include the purchase of sundry avionic equipment from Israel Aircraft Industries.

Deputy Foreign Minister Yossi Beilin wishes to expand Israeli ties to Angola. Beilin has persuaded the Defense Ministry to permit IDF soldiers to join a U.N. peacekeeping force which will patrol the country once a cease-fire between the government and UNITA is reached. After receiving government approval, Beilin submitted his proposal to Boutros-Boutros Ghali, the U.N. secretary-general.

If the U.N. accepts his offer, this will be the first time the IDF has officially served on behalf of another country. But it will be the second time that Beilin has approved sending Israelis to an African war zone. In April of last year, Beilin used Foreign Ministry funds to set up a field hospital in Somalia.

In his book *Forty Plus*, Beilin elaborated on his program to turn the IDF into a force, "to safeguard peace agreements throughout the world." It appears he is taking the first steps to turn his vision into reality.

The reader should realize that the following reports preceded government activity by months and media recognition of the issues, sometimes, by years.

In May 1994, Inside Israel *reported that the issue of water was intractable. In November, the government found a solution: it simply gave away 10 percent of the country's supply to Jordan as part of its peace treaty.*

In the same issue, Inside Israel *accurately supplied readers with precise details of Rabin's Golan withdrawal plan, a secret he was withholding from the public. Notable also was the exposure of the PLO's illegal activities at Orient House months before the abuses became a national issue.*

Finally, and most ominously, the editors collected evidence that sophisticated mind control techniques were being used against Israeli youth with disastrous consequences.

Peace Accord Reaches a Watershed

For over a year before Deputy Foreign Minister Yossi Beilin led a delegation to Oman to discuss the issue of water rights between Israel and the Palestinian entities, the government had suppressed a report on the very issue prepared in 1991 by the Institute for Strategic Studies in Tel Aviv.

The report warns that if there are separate water authorities, overpumping by the Palestinians will pollute the aquifer underlying the West Bank which supplies Israel with over 30 percent of its fresh water supply. The report recommends against a full Israeli pullback from the West Bank and suggests the boundaries of any such change be based on protecting the aquifer. Further, the report issues a strong warning not to take the water issue to international arbitration. The warning is based on the fact that water is vital to national security and Israel has never had much luck with foreign arbitrators.

Nonetheless, according to a Foreign Ministry official once close to Beilin, the deputy foreign minister has already given the water to the Palestinians (see *Inside Israel*, March 1994). His trip to Oman was mostly to ensure that no one could tamper with the promises he made in Oslo.

Beilin extracted a promise from the Clinton administration to find alternatives for Israel once it loses almost one-third of its drinking water. The Americans originally suggested building two desalinization plants, but the scheme has proven unworkable. Currently, Turkey is being persuaded to pipe massive amounts of its water resources to the Golan Heights, where it would be released into the Israeli water grid.

The plan has run into serious problems, not the least of which is that any pipeline from Turkey to Israel would have to pass through Syria. The Turks are also trying to extract a price from Israel. Both President Chaim Weizman and Foreign Minister Shimon Peres were told by the Turkish leadership that no water would flow south unless Israel agrees to lend its military hand in Turkey's war against Kurdish nationalists. So far, Israel has not agreed to the terms.

But Israel is not really thirsty yet. Beilin is almost certain to give away a good portion of the country's water, and if Israel is to replace it with the only feasible alternative (Turkish water) she may have to go to war against a long-term secret ally, the Kurds.

One of the most significant developments of 1994 was Rabin's secret agreement with the American leadership to withdraw completely from the Golan Heights. Inside Israel *was first with this story and was instrumental in exposing the alarming truth.*

Rabin Pre-Sells the Golan Heights

According to the weekly news magazine *Shishi*, Prime Minister Rabin has already cut a deal with the Syrians to withdraw from the Golan Heights. The magazine claimed it was revealing, for the first time, the details of the agreement.

According to the terms of the deal, Israel would return to the 1967 border in three stages over eight years. All Jewish settlements would fall under Syrian hegemony and the settlers would be permitted to stay under the changed rule. Naturally probably none will, but Rabin felt this approach is preferable to a forced evacuation.

The Syrians agreed to demilitarize the Golan Heights and requested that Israel do the same for areas of the Galilee bordering them. Rabin rejected the demand and Assad did not press the issue. Rabin also agreed to end the Israeli presence in the Lebanese security zone in return for Syria disarming Hizbollah and accepting the southern Lebanese army as a new division of the Lebanese army.

The package is reportedly a done deal, and Rabin has embarked on a campaign to prepare the Israeli public for the day the change is announced. Gone is Rabin's promise delivered in the Knesset by Deputy Defense Minister Mordechai Gur, that a national referendum will decide the Golan issue.

In return for his compliance, Rabin has requested some symbolic gestures from Assad. Assad has offered nothing but increased Hizbollah activity in southern Lebanon. Assad, with nothing to lose and everything to gain by his agreement with Rabin, feels under no obligation to assume a friendlier posture toward Israel.

The greatest opposition to Rabin's deal is coming from the IDF. A high level delegation of army officers submitted a report to Rabin recently which recommended against a full withdrawal from the Golan. Rabin demanded that the report be suppressed and was furious when someone leaked the officers' objections onto the front pages of weekend papers.

The morality of Israeli youth was being severely undermined in the name of selling "peace" to them.

Wherefore Israeli Youth

A report issued by Israel police and presented to the cabinet is causing great anxiety about the next generation of Israelis. The findings include a rise in violent crime of 16 percent in the past year. The conclusion reached is that the current generation of adolescents is "the most violent and egocentric in the country's history."

Certainly, the signs of change for the worse are there to see. In the past few months, two wealthy teenagers murdered a taxi driver for kicks, while a similarly well-off gang from Ramat Gan shot fourteen people in April for fun.

While LSD is passé in most of the world, Israeli youth have taken to it with a passion in the past few years. During the summer months, well-organized acid parties involving hundreds of teenagers take place in hidden locations throughout the country.

Amongst the most worrisome by-products of the new Israeli youth has been a breakdown of the country's educational system. One example is the secret Jerusalem high school organization, the Pupil Liberation Organization (PLO), which has spent the past year terrorizing teachers.

Sociologists monitoring the unwelcome transformation of Israeli teenagers into cynical delinquents have noted that such youths are not likely to make good soldiers and the affect on the IDF is going to be profound.

Brainwashing Our Youth

The Educational Psychology Department of the Tel Aviv public school system has begun a program to "train high school students to accept the peace process." According to a departmental report which preceded the implementation of the program, "A situation of drastic change leads to denial and confusion that can lead to aggression. Students who favor the change may react with euphoria that may lead to depression when their delusions are shattered."

To prevent such psychological phenomena, the program will "change perceptions about 'the enemy'" and will explain that in any peace process, there are bound to be disappointments; thus, students will not become "disoriented" by the rapid "perceptual alterations." The program has the backing of education minister Amnon Rubinstein who has approved an expansion program which will include parents and teachers from throughout the country.

While it would take the mainstream press until mid-1996 to recognize the importance of the next issue, Inside Israel *was, as usual, way ahead of the pack.*

Does Orient House Have Diplomatic Status?

Israeli policemen are complaining to the press that the PLO's East Jerusalem headquarters, Orient House, has been granted diplomatic immunity by the government. Though police minister Moshe Shachal denies the accusation, officers of his force are prevented from pursuing criminals past the gates of the building and suspected terrorists are finding sanctuary within. Further, one officer has information that the PLO is abusing the unofficial diplomatic status to stockpile huge caches of arms within its "government headquarters."

Jerusalem mayor Ehud Olmert is trying to end the special status of Orient House and has threatened to confiscate the property unless its owners pay $700,000 in back taxes. The PLO have taken the threat seriously and offered $40,000 as a down payment while its lawyers try to have the debt removed because of Orient House's "special public status."

In early June 1994 Chamish managed to interview Rabbi Uzi Meshulum in prison. While the rabbi blasted Hasidic music on a portable tape player, he spelled out a story of deep political repression. Chamish later visited Meshulum's home, which was still riddled with hundreds of bullet holes from the night Rabin and Shachal decided to put an end to him once and for all.

The following article was reprinted worldwide by the Gemini News Service in London and the aptly named American magazine, Paranoia. Despite demands by thousands of people for his release, Rabbi Meshulum still languishes in prison and the government still refuses to release the truth about the most heinous crime ever committed in Israel. The result has been the widespread alienation of Israel's large Yemenite community, the price of which has still to be paid.

Wiping Out the Stain: The Railroading of Rabbi Uzi Meshulum

Between 1948 and 1956, the highest echelons of the Israeli government and the Jewish Agency participated in the ugliest crime of the country's history. During that period, forty-five hundred infants and young children, all immigrants, were kidnapped and sold to adoptive parents abroad. The children were taken from Jewish Agency child welfare centers, from clinics in immigrant camps (*maabarot*), and even directly from maternity wards. The parents were told that their children had died and were issued forged death certificates.

Those parents who sought their children's graves failed, for none existed. In fact, the children were sold for $5,000 each to childless couples, mostly in America. There is evidence that some of the children were sold for medical experiments or strange cult practices.

The roots of the crime lay in the thousands of Holocaust orphans brought to Israel in the late 1940s. Sincere American couples requested the right to adopt indigent children and raise them in dignity. The Israeli government was reluctant to agree to the many requests, desiring instead to populate the new nation with European Jews.

But the temptation to earn money selling babies may have proved too much for the new nation, which sorely needed income to pay for defense and, ironically, immigrant absorption. At some point in time, a decision was made at the highest levels to substitute orphan European children with dark Yemenite babies whose parents were very much alive. The total income derived from the black market babies was some $25 million, a figure equivalent today to several hundreds of millions of dollars.

Naturally the disappearance of thousands of babies did not go unnoticed and the parents tried to recover them. Some newcomers with enough sophistication and knowledge of Hebrew turned to the press. Throughout the 1950s numerous reports of babies disappearing were published in the local papers.

Any parent who objected too much was treated brutally. Today's mayor of Rosh Haayin, Yigal Yosef, recalls how his sister was stolen shortly after her birth. His mother made a screaming exhibition of herself at the maternity hospital demanding to see either her live baby or the corpse. She was taken by the police, beaten, warned never to open her mouth again, and thrown wounded from a moving car onto the street outside her house. Such incidents were commonplace in the 1950s.

In 1967, journalist Uri Avineri exposed the scandal in his controversial publication, *Haolam Hazeh*. Shortly after, he was the target for assassination. Fortunately for him, his intended killer's gun jammed and Avineri captured him. He was exposed as an agent for the Shabak, the country's internal security apparatus.

Avineri's successor in trying to expose the hideous crime was

a young rabbi, Uzi Meshulum. In the early 1970s, Meshulum began gathering the names of the kidnapped children in an attempt
to trace them. He was well placed to break through the bureaucratic silence on the issue. As a soldier, he led some of the IDF's
most secret operations. (He lost his body hair in an attack on a
Syrian biological warfare center). Using his contacts in the security services while recruiting new agents, many of Yemenite background, Meshulum infiltrated deep into the cover-up of the affair
and became the driving force behind a lobbying campaign aimed
at pressuring the government to open a commission of inquiry
into the kidnappings.

In 1985, at the initiative of Knesset members Shlomo
Virshuvsky and Dov Shilansky, the Knesset's interior committee
began a preliminary investigation of the charges. At this point,
the veil of secrecy was momentarily lifted when Avigdor Peer, who
was the deputy head of the new immigrants division of the Ministry of Welfare during the period of the kidnappings, broke his
thirty-year silence. He informed the committee that numerous
illegal adoptions took place and pointed to the:

> involvement of the government establishment in the affair as
> expressed by the allotment, according to the recognized rela-
> tive power of the political parties, of quantities of children for
> the purpose of adoption to four women's organizations associ-
> ated with the members of the government coalition; Naamat
> of Labor, Aguda Women of Agudat Yisrael, Emuna Women of
> the National Religious Party and the General Zionists Women's
> Organization.

As a result of this and other testimony the committee recommended a public inquiry into the affair; the Knesset turned down
the recommendation.

And with good reason. Peer's testimony implicated one cabinet minister, Dr. Yosef Burg, who was interior minister for part of
the time during the kidnappings, of being a perpetrator of the

crime. Burg's son Avraham is today a member of the Labor government.

But Burg was not the only member of the government who likely knew that the kidnappings were taking place. In order for an operation of this scope and profit to succeed, the health, welfare, defense, and interior ministries had to be involved as did the Jewish Agency, which supplied many of the children. None of this could have been kept secret from the prime minister during most of the period of the crime, David Ben Gurion.

While the kidnapping and illegal adoption operation was taking place Amos Ben Gurion, the prime minister's son, was the police minister, former president Chaim Herzog was head of military intelligence, and today's foreign minister, Shimon Peres, was a close aide of Ben Gurion in charge of arms acquisitions. While much of the profits of the baby trade were funneled into the parties and pockets of the kidnappers, much undoubtedly went toward the purchase of arms.

Meshulum's campaign seemed to have borne fruit in 1988 when the Shamir government appointed a commission of inquiry, led by Judge Moshe Shalgi, to get to the bottom of the matter. The commission's early finding was that "only" some 650 babies had been kidnapped and sold illegally. In the six years since the commission has theoretically been at work seeking the truth, no further revelations have been forthcoming.

However, Meshulum would not give up the fight and over time his work earned him a dedicated congregation of hundreds and sympathizers numbering in the many tens of thousands. This congregation would later be described by the government and media as a cult, and Meshulum painted as an Israeli version of David Koresh.

By 1992 Meshulum had begun videotaping and distributing cassettes of parents who had been threatened by paid killers, of journalists who were told their jobs were at stake if they reported on the affair, and of witnesses who had participated in the crime and could no longer live with themselves.

He also began naming names of the criminals, and they are a "who's who" of early Zionist legend. They include Labor's finance minister and kingpin dealmaker Pinchas Sapir, who was chairman of the Jewish Agency during the kidnappings. Also implicated is Moshe Rivlin, the current chairman of the Jewish National Fund; and Moshe Ben Maimon, treasurer of the Jewish Agency. Displaying almost suicidal courage, he named the Shabak agent in charge of suppressing the crime, Ilan Raz.

Meshulum was not alone in exposing the crime. The ultra-Orthodox sect Satmar published a book called *Genocide in Israel* which documented the tragedy. The Shabak threatened the sect and mostly succeeded in suppressing the book. However since 1993 when reports that Yemen was going to release its Jews to Israel first appeared, the sect has been sending agents to Yemen to redirect them to New York.

On March 9 of this year, Meshulum released a magazine that was the most detailed exposé of the crime to date. Two weeks later a "contractor" was sent to provoke an incident. The "contractor" dumped cement in Meshulum's sewage system and returned the next day to try it again. This time he was stopped by Meshulum's students. An army of 250 police and Shabak units descended on his property to settle the problem. Such a concentration of sharpshooters, sappers, helicopters, attack dogs, etc., is rarely gathered for an operation against terrorists in Lebanon or Gaza, let alone to help out in a dispute with a rude contractor.

Meshulum and his followers were under siege. Anyone who left the property was beaten and arrested. Six weeks later, a thousand police and Shabak officers descended on Meshulum at the order of the prime minister and Police Minister Moshe Shachal. A nineteen-year-old boy, who the police claimed had shot at a helicopter, was killed by a police sharpshooter. Witnesses to the shooting insist the boy was unarmed. The boy was not fatally shot and a Hebrew University historian, Natan Shipris, left the property in order to persuade the police to call an ambulance. He was bound, dragged 150 yards, kicked mercilessly, and arrested.

An hour and a half later, the boy bled to death.

The next day Meshulum and his followers at the property were in custody. Meshulum was beaten for seven hours and about one-third of his congregation suffered the same fate. Meanwhile, 150 sympathizers of Meshulum's cause were rounded up across the country and arrested.

Meshulum and his closest followers were charged with fifteen different crimes, including attempted murder and conspiracy. The government hopes that by imprisoning them all it can wipe this ugliest of stains out of the country's fabric. However, the stain may prove to be indelible.

Media manipulation was the name of the game in the Rabin–Peres government. Peres' buddy, the powerful French media magnate Jean Friedman, financed and organized the rally at which Rabin was assassinated. There is no denying that the Peres-aligned Frenchman was the financier of the campaign to brainwash the Israeli public into accepting a very dirty peace.

Resentment of Brainwashing Touches IDF

One of the hidden clauses of Oslo was a commitment by Deputy Foreign Minister Yossi Beilin to mount a sophisticated promotional campaign to convince Israelis to accept the peace program. The task fell to longtime Shimon Peres backer Jean Friedman to fund the campaign.

Friedman is the driving force behind a number of schemes. It was he who gathered a group of ancient generals, including former Tel Aviv mayor Shlomo Lahat, to demonstrate in favor of the government's policy. And he hired Lahat to head a "charitable" fund called "Ifshar" to plaster the street corners and billboards of the country with posters reading, "We Want Peace."

Likud MK Ron Nachman has protested the method of the poster campaign and the source of the funding in the Knesset.

Nachman claims the posters employ "deceptive subliminal messages that border on the hypnotic."

Nachman was joined by Tsomet MK Moshe Peled in his objections to the kidnapping of Hizbollah sheikh El Mustapha Dirani. The day before the kidnapping operation deep in the Syrian-controlled Bekaa Valley, two IDF soldiers were killed at a Gaza border post. In a blatant breach of the autonomy agreement, the Palestinian police refused to hunt the murderers, saying as far as they were concerned the murders were "a closed case."

This incident soured the public on the peace process and the government responded with an operation kept ready for just such a contingency. The sheikh was captured supposedly to advance the return from captivity of Ron Arad, who was a Hizbollah prisoner of war over a decade ago and has since either died or been transferred to Iran.

Peled and Nachman objected to the cynical use of the IDF to quell public anger over the autonomy accords. Other observers noted that the helicopter attack in the Bekaa could not possibly have succeeded without the compliance of Syria. One insider at the Foreign Ministry said that "Syria agreed not to shoot down the IDF helicopters as part of the overall understanding with it that Israel will give up the Golan Heights in the very near future. The Syrians were willing to bail out Rabin's government to keep their prospects of a total withdrawal alive."

Chapter Five

July 1994

While Rabin's secret ties were to London and New York, Peres' masters were European. His New World Order machinations reached an apex with his sellout of Jerusalem to the Vatican. When Inside Israel reported the ultimate betrayal of the Jewish capital, it was the Jewish readers who considered the story too fantastic to be believed. On the other hand, the report was responsible for increasing Christian readership. They sensed the veracity of the information immediately.

Eight months later the radio station Arutz Sheva uncovered a cable from the Israeli Embassy in Rome to the Foreign Ministry in Jerusalem detailing the Jerusalem sellout and Haaretz reprinted it on its front page. Inside Israel's "fantastic" claims were once again verified, as was the information provided in the story on Teddy Kollek dividing Jerusalem in the December 1993 issue.

Meanwhile, a majority of the newsletter's readers were now Christian and on four continents. The editors, quite incidentally, were providing information that fulfilled prophecy. As a result, they found themselves speaking before Christian groups in Israel and Britain more often than the Jewish audiences they felt sure would be their natural readership when the publication began.

The editors were somewhat bemused by the enthusiastic response they elicited every time they spoke before Christian crowds. They quickly grew to admire the hard working, decent life-style of their new adherents and especially their deep concern for Israel. Somewhat disconcerting was their feeling that these Christians were far better friends of Israel than the minions of liberal Jews everywhere who were too blind and ignorant to see that Israel was headed for destruction.

The downside, both editors agreed, was the underlying and

occasionally overt belief that Jews must accept Jesus Christ as the Messiah. Many readers are surprised to learn that Barry Chamish and Joel Bainerman are both proud, secular Jews with no alliance to any political movement and no ideological backers. The editors' answer to the issue of differences between Jews and Christians is that when the Messiah arrives, the truth will be known. In some miraculous fashion, both religions will be proven right.

Peres Sells Jerusalem to the Vatican

Foreign Minister Shimon Peres' plans for Jerusalem's future are slowly being exposed and, with his back to the wall, he has been engaging in transparent lies.

The first occurred after PLO chairman Yasser Arafat, during a speech in Johannesburg, revealed the existence of a letter from Peres to the Norwegian foreign minister sent in October 1993, committing Israel to respect PLO governing institutions in Jerusalem. Peres denied that such a letter existed, much to the chagrin of cabinet whip Moshe Shachal, who transmitted Peres' message to the Knesset and was furious when the government later admitted that such a letter was actually sent.

In response to the revelation of the letter, Peres told the Knesset forum, "If you are insinuating that we would ever divide Jerusalem, that's an ugly slander." In Peres-speak, this means that he is planning to divide Jerusalem. That fact was revealed in another letter, this one sent to Pope John Paul II.

A close friend of Peres', the French intellectual Mark Halter, told the weekly *Shishi* that in May he delivered a letter from Peres to the pope which outlined the foreign minister's plans for Jerusalem. According to Halter, "Peres offered to hand over sovereignty of Jerusalem's Old City to the Vatican."

Halter elaborated on the plan: "The city will stay the capital of Israel but will be administered by the Vatican. The city will have an Israeli mayor and a Palestinian mayor, both under orders from the Holy See. The program was originally submitted to the

Vatican by Peres two years ago, just before the Oslo talks began."

The Vaticanization plan was presented to the PLO during the Oslo negotiations. Just before the signing of the Declaration of Principles, Arafat agreed not to oppose the plan. The plan also has the support of a number of influential Palestinian intellectuals who were consulted, including Professor Edward Said.

The Peres plan calls for the extraterritoriality of the Old City and the airport at Atarot, which will become an international meeting center.

The plan was first published in the Italian newspaper *La Stampa* on September 10, 1993, three days before Rabin met Arafat in Washington. At the time, Peres ordered the Foreign Ministry to deny that such a program existed. Today, Foreign Ministry workers are not issuing denials and are privately confirming the existence of such a plan.

Further details of the plan call for Jerusalem to become the second Vatican of the world, with all three major religions having some degree of autonomy but under the authority of the Vatican. A Palestinian state will emerge in confederation with Jordan with its religious capital being Jerusalem but its administrative capital situated elsewhere, possibly Nablus.

A Foreign Ministry source believes the plan is a good one. He stresses that Israel's ties to the Catholic world will lead to trade, tourism, and prosperity. Further, with a strong governing authority, future disputes between Israelis and Arabs will be easily resolved.

Despite denials by the government that the future of Jerusalem is being negotiated, facts on the ground are quite different. The PLO's Jerusalem chief, Faisal el Husseini, informed Police Minister Shachal that before the signing of the Declaration of Principles, the government made a secret deal with the PLO committing itself to freezing housing construction in the city. On September 23, 1993, Tzomet leader Raful Eitan demanded from Peres that he explain all the terms of the agreement but Peres denied that such a deal had been cut. Nonetheless, not one new neighborhood has been constructed in the past year.

Husseini has also announced that talks over the future of Jerusalem between the PLO and the government are being conducted in Bethlehem. Meanwhile a forum called, not very ironically, Metropolitan Jerusalem, under the auspices of former mayor Teddy Kollek, "is preparing plans for the canonization of Jerusalem" which the government is submitting for negotiation in Bethlehem.

The IDF is actively changing its defense positions around the capital, literally returning to the 1948 lines. Four border posts surround the city and Jewish residents coming into neighborhoods such as Ramot and Pisgat Zeev from over the Green Line must now present identification papers before being permitted to travel home. Economics Minister Shimon Sheetret was not told of the new arrangement and was furious to be stopped at a "border post in Jerusalem."

Sheetret was not informed that three weeks before the Cairo agreement was signed, Peres and Arafat met in Bucharest, Rumania, with the Iranian foreign minister and there decided on a number of fateful issues. Arafat was given pledges that the Al Aqsa mosque will become independent of Israel and that he will be allowed to visit before the change of status. Ultimately, the sovereignty of Jerusalem will be shared by the PLO and Israel. Peres also agreed to increase the size of the Palestinian police force to include five hundred Sudanese trained by Islamic fundamentalists, and acquiesced completely on the right of return for all Palestinians to all currently disputed areas including Jerusalem.

Border patrol units are presently repositioning themselves in a circle around Jerusalem whose circumference is formed by the towns of Tzur Hadassah, Bet Guvrin, and Kibbutz Maale Khamisha, or the pre-1967 deployment. In a meeting between the commander of the border guards and police officials, resident leaders warned them that the new orders suggest "that a deal has already been cut with the PLO over Jerusalem and it's about to go into force."

*Israel's negotiating partners discovered that they got more after
delivering violent messages. When negotiations stalled, a well-placed
bomb got them back on track. But who would have believed that even
"moderate" Jordan was not above using this bloody strategy?*

*The following report is yet another story the mainstream media
missed, but* Inside Israel *didn't.*

Jordan Responsible for Recent Bombings

The government of Jordan either permitted or ordered the two
April car bombings in Afula and Hadera which killed thirteen
Israelis, mostly school children. After the Afula slaughter, the leader
of Hamas in Jordan promised four more suicide bombings and
true to his word, the Hadera explosion took place on April 15.

The Jordanians apparently informed Washington of its intentions and literally just as the bomb exploded in Hadera, the House
Foreign Affairs Committee heard an appeal from Dan Kretzer,
deputy secretary of state for Middle Eastern Affairs, to increase
aid to Jordan immediately in order to draw it into the peace process.

While Congress was debating increasing U.S. aid, Prime Minister Rabin was publicly threatening action against Jordan, and
Foreign Minister Peres announced that he held the country responsible for the recent car bombings.

Most analysts assumed Rabin and Peres blamed the Jordanian government for not putting a leash on Hamas activities. In
fact, before the April bombings no Jordanian group had taken
responsibility for an Israeli bombing in years.

On April 23 Secretary of State Warren Christopher met King
Hussein in London to "iron out differences with Jordan." Jordan
was upset by the American-led embargo on her Red Sea port of
Aqaba which began in the wake of the Gulf War of 1990. Since
then, to prevent the smuggling of arms into Iraq all ships bound
for Jordan had been stopped and searched. The Jordanians be-

lieved that the costly embargo's real purpose was not to prevent arms smuggling, but to pressure Hussein into cutting a peace deal with Israel. By the end of the meeting Christopher had agreed to Hussein's demand that American searches of ships coming into Aqaba port be stopped and that Lloyd's of London inspectors replace the American sailors.

After the London meeting, all Hamas threats against Israel ceased, as did further car bombings. Clearly, Hussein could turn Hamas on and off at will. The purpose of the Afula and Hadera attacks was not to avenge the Hebron massacre of February to March, but to further Jordanian diplomatic aims.

Jordan's use of hard ball tactics and the murder of a dozen young Israelis did not dismay the Israeli government for long. In late May Rabin met Hussein in London, and on June 2 Peres flew to London and boarded another plane to a secret destination to meet the monarch.

Within two weeks Hussein was in Washington and was rewarded for his wise diplomacy with the cancellation of $700 million in debts to the American government. Within days a summit was planned between Israel and Jordan in Aqaba.

The role London is playing in the peace process has been decidedly downplayed. The Oslo talks were initiated in London after discussions were held between current PLO "finance minister" Abu Abas and the Israeli left-wing academic Yair Hirschfeld in November of 1992. Also present in London at that same time was Deputy Foreign Minister Yossi Beilin, who reported the meetings to Prime Minister Rabin and recommended pursuing a peace based on them.

In late May Beilin was back in London and this time he secured an agreement from Foreign Secretary Douglas Hurd to end the twelve-year-old British arms embargo against Israel. It is not understood why Beilin was chosen to negotiate the end of the embargo, though clearly his quiet but close ties to the British were a deciding factor.

While Peres was left out of the Oslo track, he was determined to be the hero that brought peace with Syria. The relentless competition between Rabin and Peres reduced the value and price of the Golan Heights to nothing. Syria could have them if it signed a peace treaty right away.

Bypassing Rabin

Foreign Minister Peres is desperately trying to lead the peace talks with Syria and is attempting to bypass and then overwhelm Prime Minister Rabin's own diplomacy.

In May, Peres begged French president Françoise Mitterand to open channels for him with Syria, claiming American interest in the peace process was waning. Shortly afterward, he begged the Turkish leadership to use its good offices to help him out.

The situation has grown so absurd that Elyakim Rubinstein, head of the Israeli delegation to the Washington peace talks, told reporters that "the Syrians told me that Peres is taking extraordinary measures to arrange a meeting between him and Syrian officials." Among the measures mentioned were appealing to "international businessmen" to intervene on his behalf.

In anticipation of success, Peres has ordered workers at the Foreign Ministry to prepare a complete peace program to present to the Syrians, which will be more palatable than the Rabin approach.

Meanwhile RIA, the Soviet government information agency, has reported that secret talks are taking place between Israel and the U.S. whose aim is the immediate breakup of settlements in the Golan and the territories, to be followed by the handing over of the emptied lands to the Syrians and Palestinians.

An Israeli source confirms the meetings and says that they are taking place at the State Department with the Israeli negotiators being responsible to Deputy Foreign Minister Yossi Beilin.

While exposing more Arye Deri ties to Rabin's p
issue Inside Israel *introduced its readers to the '*₁
first time. Two years later the party would win four seats ₁
and join the Likud coalition. At the time, the other English
*media dismissed the significance of the faction. Finally, oppos*₁
the suicidal "peace" process was being heard from within the Labor
Party.

The Deri-Sheves-Ramon-Histadrut Scam

Shimon Sheves, director-general of the Prime Minister's Office, has filed a police complaint against parties who sent a message to Labor Party activists via the party's computers. He is also pressing the prime minister to clamp down on use of the computer lines.

The message accused Sheves of cutting a deal "at a Tel Aviv hotel room" with Shas leader Arye Deri and Haim Ramon to win the leadership of the national labor union, the Histadrut. The Labor leadership got wind of the plan and, according to Deri, offered him about $3 million to support their campaign over Ramon's.

Control of the Histadrut is a key to Labor's power, and the party spent $800 million of government funds upping workers' salaries and perks in the three months leading to the election. Housing Minister Benjamin Ben Eliezer contributed millions of dollars to Arab town councils in return for securing votes, a process Israel Television called "bribery."

In addition, Haim Ramon accused Finance Minister Avraham Shohat of deliberately withholding the extent of Histadrut debts from the public during the same period. Nonetheless, Ramon (Rabin's appointment as health minister, who later left Labor when his program for a national health plan was abandoned by the prime minister) wrested power from Labor for the first time in the union's history.

Shas did not run its own candidates in the election, choosing to ally itself with Ramon. The total cost of the alliance is still not

, but Ramon did funnel about half a million dollars into the Shas newspaper for "current and future advertising," a deal first revealed by Likud MK Michael Eitan.

Both Ramon and Sheves are tied to Deri in crime, a fact which Labor exploited in national advertising. Ramon received about $50,000 from Moshe Reich for acting as attorney in the sale of a mortgage bank. Reich was later accused by the police of giving Deri a $100,000 bribe to purchase an apartment. The police did not elaborate on the motive for the bribe, but later charges against Reich for smuggling $7.9 million worth of electronic goods into the country were mysteriously dropped in the midst of his trial and the alleged bribe did not appear in Deri's indictment.

Sheves was a central figure in a land scam—an Israeli version of Whitewater. In 1989 Deri purchased plots of farm land in Har Shmuel near Jerusalem and used his political influence to trade the worthless property for urban land with approval for development. The bureaucratic exchange was highly profitable and was accomplished with the influence of Sheves, the prime minister's aide for urban settlement.

While the Deri investigation continued Har Shmuel was closed to development. Two weeks after Ramon's election the property received a building permit, providing the long awaited opportunity for development and profit.

A common feeling is that Sheves knows Rabin's days are numbered and wants to ally himself with the next Labor leader. Ramon will likely use the Histadrut chairmanship to launch a leadership bid for Labor, which has an excellent chance of succeeding. However, former Rabin aide Haim Assa claims Rabin was in on Ramon's campaign from the beginning and was in constant contact with Ramon during the last days of the election.

In response to Ramon's challenge, Yossi Beilin is making a bid to lead the left-wing faction of the party in alliance with Meretz, while a group of "hawkish" MKs, as yet leaderless, has formed still another faction called Third Way. It is trying to form a pact with moderate Likud MKs to slow down, if not halt, Rabin's peace process, which it believes is leading to the downfall of the party.

Rabin is facing a wave of defections from his own party. The seven Labor MKs behind the Third Way have signed a letter warning Rabin that they will fight any withdrawal on the Golan. They are Avigdor Kahalani, Gedalia Gal, Eli Goldschmidt, Raanan Cohen, Emanuel Zisman, Yaacov Shefi, and Yossi Vanunu. Kahalani has gone a step further than the rest, announcing that he would quit Labor over the Golan issue. Yossi Vanunu's stand is believed to have played a role in the government's decision to have him prosecuted for bribery committed in 1991.

The international powerbrokers were blatant and clumsy in their plot to destroy Rwanda. But because of world public apathy, the plans worked anyway. The World Bank and International Monetary Fund (IMF) indebted the country and forced the rulers to accept a one-crop economy. The destruction of the peasant class and a sudden inability to feed itself was Rwanda's inevitable fate. Rising tribal tension lead the United Nations to send troops. Henry Kissinger and Lord Carrington arrived in Rwanda to mediate an end to the crisis. Two days after their departure a plane crash killed the country's leader and massacres followed. U.N. troops which could have stopped the slaughter were ordered not to. A million refugees streamed onto the shores of a lake in nearby Zaire. The U.N. forced the pitiful Rwandans away from the lake, whence they died of thirst by the tens of thousands. And who played a secret role in this NWO atrocity? Why, Yossi Beilin, of course.

Beilin Helps His African Friends

Deputy Foreign Minister Yossi Beilin told the Knesset Foreign Affairs Committee that "in the past two months Israel has been secretly helping two African countries settle internal differences."

Beilin did not name which countries, but they are most likely Angola and Rwanda. In May Beilin submitted a formal request to

U.N. secretary-general Boutros-Boutros Ghali to permit Israeli soldiers to join U.N. peacekeeping troops that he expected would be called to the country.

Israel took an active role in Rwanda previous to the massacres in the country, supplying the government with significant amounts of heavy armor and weapons. Once the slaughter of May began, the government slapped an embargo on further sales.

The Foreign Ministry explained: "Weapons were sold to a legal government fighting terrorists operating from outside the country." The implication was that the Foreign Ministry had no idea the arms would contribute to one of the biggest massacres of the century.

October 1994

> *Another murderous explosion in Buenos Aires and another cover-up. All in the name of not souring the Israeli public on Syria and thus endangering their willingness to give up the Golan Heights for a treaty with a brutal dictatorship. Why the two blasts occurred has never been solved by this newsletter or anyone else. But Syria, apparently, had a very important message for Rabin.*

Israel Covers Up Buenos Aires Blast

The Israeli government is covering up for the perpetrators of the latest Buenos Aires explosion which killed over one hundred people, just as it did twenty-eight months previously when a blast at the Israeli Embassy left twenty-nine dead.

In the wake of the first outrage, facts collected by an Argentine television investigation and by journalist Nurit Steinberg pointed the finger of blame at Syria. Argentinian president Carlos Menem was born in Syria and maintains close ties to Syrian-funded terrorist groups active in his country. Just before the explosion he illegally granted citizenship to the Syrian terrorist

Monzer Al-Kassar, who the FBI suspects of planning the *Achille Lauro* takeover and the PanAm explosion over Lockerbie as well as playing a central role in Iran-Contra.

The Israeli Embassy filmed the license number of the suicide bomb vehicle and traced it to a car dealer who claimed he had sold the car three weeks before to "an Arab with a Brazilian passport." The bank notes used to pay for the car were traced to Syrian banks.

Although fully informed, the Israeli government did not attempt to name the real perpetrators, preferring to hint that Iran was responsible. This infuriated Israel's ambassador to Argentina, Yaacov Shefi, who publicly declared that "Jerusalem was not interested in finding those responsible for fear of a diplomatic embarrassment." The embarrassment he was referring to was that Syria ordered the blast which killed over two dozen Jews.

Menem's ties are not just to Syria; they extend to Syrian ally Libya. The PanAm 103 explosion was reportedly orchestrated by Al-Kassar in concert with Syria and Libya. In 1989 Libyan president Muamar Ghaddafi donated $4.5 million to Menem's election campaign. A week before the first blast, the Libyan dictator demanded the money back. A few days later Menem asked the Organization of Non-Aligned Nations to back sanctions against the U.S. for attacks against Libya. Despite the gesture, Menem would still not return Ghaddafi's money. The bomb at the Israeli Embassy exploded shortly after his last refusal.

Menem has turned Argentina into a haven for international terrorists who are funneled to the country via Libya, Algeria, and Syria. The terrorists responsible for the Bologna train station explosion which killed eighty-nine people have found a sanctuary in Buenos Aires. Menem has turned down all requests from Italy for their return.

Quickly after the most recent attack, Argentinian authorities arrested an Arab with a Brazilian passport. His suspected role in the explosion and his judicial fate have since disappeared from the media. Far more serious are claims by Israeli Embassy staff in

Chile that they had received intelligence warnings that a major attack was planned, after which no action was taken.

Israel is also paying no attention to data being gathered by journalist Walter Guber. He has traced responsibility for the blast to the former chief of Menem's personal security, who is holed up in a bunker under a villa close to Menem's home. An Argentinian judge is now examining the evidence, but as Shlomo Slotzky of *Shishi* notes, "Also in this case, Israel is showing no interest and is not asking for details."

The blast coincided precisely with the opening of peace talks between Israel and Jordan. On the same day, attacks against the lives of Jordanian cabinet ministers were foiled in Amman. Buenos Aires was Syria's way of expressing disapproval of the separate negotiations. Prime Minister Rabin and Foreign Minister Peres are aware of the implications for peace of Syrian involvement and once again are covering up the facts.

There was more to the peace treaty with Jordan than most people knew. Inside Israel dug deep until it found the whole story.

Giving in to Jordan

The Israeli-Jordanian peace accord did not catch close observers by surprise. The current deal between Israel and Jordan was the result of a secret trip last November by Foreign Minister Shimon Peres to Jordan.

Among the terms of peace with Jordan, Israel promised to accept Jordanian sovereignty over a disputed 380 square kilometers of land in the Arava Wadi area, or about one-third of all agricultural land in the Dead Sea–Red Sea rift. Further, King Hussein was promised five square kilometers of the resort city of Eilat. Peres also committed Israel to intervene militarily if the Hashemite kingdom was ever attacked by a third party. Jordan did not make the same commitment to Israel. Another clause in the treaty commits Israel to use its influence in Congress to have Jordanian debts to the U.S. forgiven.

Rabin's reaction to the Jordanian land grab was predictable. He told journalists in New York, "What's a few kilometers compared to peace with Jordan?"

It took two years but Inside Israel *finally risks losing credibility with its "conventional" readership and openly espouses an anti-NWO editorial bias. The transformation is innocent enough. The* Jerusalem Post *is widely viewed as an independent, right-wing paper. The editors found ties linking it to Henry Kissinger and thus to globalist policy.*

The editors made a decision to release the most disturbing information it had gathered on the Rabin–Kissinger connection as relevant background to the story. From this point on, Inside Israel *names its enemies and becomes the only publication devoted to exposing the covert plot by the world's powerbrokers to weaken and then eliminate Israel. That is, unless U.N. troops don't step in just in the nick of time and extract major concessions in Jerusalem.*

Who Is Running Israel's Foreign Policy?

The consensus in the Israeli journalistic and diplomatic community is that the *Jerusalem Post* is a right-wing paper dedicated to felling the Labor Party and its allies. Yet the background of the owner of the paper, Conrad Black, CEO of the Hollinger Corporation, would suggest a very different perspective.

Black is a long-standing member of two of the world's leading "globalist" organizations, the Council on Foreign Relations and the Trilateral Commission, both of which are believed to play a major behind-the-scenes role in American and world politics.

According to a 1993 article in New York-based *Vanity Fair* magazine, the Hollinger Corporation is one of the most prominent clients of Kissinger Associates, the high-powered consulting firm established by the former secretary of state. Other clients include

Chase Manhattan Bank, owned by the Rockefeller family, as well as a number of major oil companies.

Kissinger set the precedent for diplomatic pressure on Israel to secede lands won in war and is assumed to have had a decisive influence on Prime Minister Yitzhak Rabin's original accession to power. Last month it was Kissinger who presented Rabin and Foreign Minister Peres with the UNESCO Peace Prize in Paris.

According to the Egyptian writer Mohammed Heykel, quoting Syrian sources, one of the terms of the American arms airlift to Israel during the Yom Kippur War, which Kissinger delayed for nine days until Israel's situation was desperate, was that Golda Meir resign as prime minister in favor of Rabin. Up to that time Rabin had never been a member of the Knesset and was far down on the Labor Party list. After the war, Meir appointed Rabin minister of labor and shortly afterward backed his candidacy for party leadership. To this day, Rabin owes his political power to Dr. K.

Six months ago, Defense Minister Rabin approved a significant arms sales to Rwanda. Three days before the Rwanda civil war erupted, Kissinger and Lord Carrington flew to Rwanda on an undisclosed diplomatic mission. Upon returning to the U.S., Foreign Minister Peres was summoned to meet Kissinger in a Manhattan restaurant. Peres was on his way to a diplomatic tour of South America and took a 5,000-mile detour to meet Kissinger for six hours.

The day preceding Henry Kissinger's awarding of the UNESCO Peace Prize to Foreign Minister Peres and Prime Minister Rabin in Paris was a busy one for Israeli foreign policy. Peres was in the Azerbaijan Republic signing a joint agreement to fight Islamic fundamentalism, while his deputy Yossi Beilin was in New York securing U.N. Secretary-General Boutros-Boutros Ghali's approval of the placement of Israeli troops to keep the peace in Angola. The two diplomats also reached a rather surprising preliminary agreement to move both the offices of the United Nations Relief Works Agency (UNRWA) and UNESCO from Europe to the Gaza Strip.

Beilin's stated policy of turning the IDF into an international peace army appears to be right on schedule. Israeli troops are now in Rwanda and Beilin has offered them for peacekeeping functions if America attacks Haiti.

Although considered at most an elder statesman by political analysts, in fact, it appears that Dr. Kissinger has an enormous and unexplainable influence on Israeli foreign policy.

By the fall of 1994, one year after the Oslo agreements were signed, the first group of IDF officers threatened mutiny. Following them, the heads of the intelligence services were abandoning ship.

Mutiny in the Intelligence Services

Israel's intelligence leaders, realizing the implications of the peace process on the country's security, are quitting at an alarming rate. First to go was an unnamed divisional commander of the Mossad, who held a general's rank and was described as "the second

Yitzhak Rabin with Henry Kissinger, 1974

highest Mossad officer, after the head of the service."

Next to quit was Yaacov Perry, the head of the Shabak (Israel's internal intelligence service). Prime Minister Rabin reportedly begged him to stay, fearing a security breakdown during the autonomy process. The chief spook refuted the appeal and several top officers are reportedly following him out.

Chapter Six

January 1995

While Rabin is trying to persuade Congress to place American troops on the abandoned Golan Heights, Peres is offering the scraps to Europe. Japan sees the race is on and puts in its own dibs on the territory.

Golan for Sale

Three countries are vying for the right to place their troops on the Golan Heights in the wake of an Israeli withdrawal.

The United States is taking far-reaching measures to this end, even soliciting support from liberal American Jewish rabbis to push this position from their pulpits. In an odd and unpleasant twist of history, Shimon Peres actually invited German chancellor Helmut Kohl to place his country's soldiers on the Heights. In the same week as the Peres request to Kohl, Japan announced that it was considering putting its troops on the Golan.

Peres' request to Kohl was part of a very strange deal with Germany. In exchange for Israel recruiting the American Jewish Congress to lobby for Germany's inclusion in the U.N. Security Council, Germany agreed to push Israel as an associate member of the European Community. The Congress admitted that their efforts were coordinated with the Foreign Ministry and Peres told the German media during an August visit to Bonn that Israel would support German entry into the Security Council.

While Israel's efforts have so far gone nowhere, Germany's are bearing fruit. Both France and Britain dropped previous objections to Israel being a partner in the European Community's research and development programs.

The greatest opposition to withdrawal is coming from the IDF. A high-level delegation of army officers recently submitted a report to Rabin which recommended against a full withdrawal from the Golan Heights. Rabin demanded that the report be suppressed and was furious at a leak that appeared on the front pages of all the weekend papers. His public response was that he "isn't required to listen to his senior officers' advice."

However, before any withdrawal can be anticipated, Israel must acquiesce to Syria's demand that it sign the Nuclear Non-Proliferation Treaty and thus open the Dimona reactor to international inspectors who will demand an end to the Israeli nuclear program. According to well-informed security sources, Rabin is prepared to trade all of the Golan Heights for an agreement with Syria and throw in Israel's nuclear option to boot.

Rabin's willingness flies in the face of a rather disturbing fact. This year Syria purchased a 27-MW nuclear reactor from China capable of producing its own atomic weaponry.

The American, German, and Japanese troops might someday face a nuclear-armed Syria, while purportedly defending Israel's northern border.

The following article impressed the editor of the New York Jewish Post. *He reprinted it, and reaction was such that the editors were offered their own column called, not unexpectedly,* Inside Israel. *In one stroke, readership increased by tens of thousands.*

Closing Down the Media

While the world press has expressed outrage at the closing of such Palestinian newspapers as *An-Nahar* and *Akhbar al-Balad* by Yasser Arafat for opposing his policies, a far greater purge is taking place within Israel without any outside notice.

As a direct result of exposing the less savory side of the peace process one Israeli paper after another has been closed, supposedly for financial reasons. But as Reno Tsror, former editor of the weekly *Shishi*, the latest victim of the closures notes, "Well before they shut us down, there were offers to buy us. Even after the closure offers came in, but our publishers wouldn't negotiate with anyone."

First to go in the campaign to suppress free expression was *Monitin*, a glossy monthly known for its superb diplomatic and military intelligence. It was *Monitin* which published Mubarak's threat to rearm the Sinai if Rabin didn't honor agreements cut by Peres and the PLO before he assumed leadership of the Labor Party, and it was *Monitin* which covered Rabin's first offers to Syria to forego the Golan Heights for a peace agreement.

Next out was the staff of *Vreyma*, a Russian-language paper owned by *Maariv* whose editorial policy was opposed to the Israel-PLO accords from their conception. As one ex-staffer explained, "Rabin called Yaacov Nimrodi [*Maariv*'s owner] personally and asked him to act. He then fired all the journalists and sold the paper."

Eight months ago, *Haolam Hazeh* and *Hadashot* closed down. Since the 1960s *Haolam Hazeh* had been the primary source of investigative journalism and is credited with first breaking the story of the stolen Yemenite children of the 1950s. *Hadashot*, owned by *Haaretz*, was the only paper to expose the fraud of the 1992 elections when Shimon Peres made a deal with the PLO to recruit Israeli Arab voters on behalf of Labor in return for a future state.

The final blow came in August when *Shishi*, *Haolam Hazeh*'s successor, had its life cut short. Among its last cover stories was the revelation that Rabin had agreed to stop Israel's nuclear program for a Syrian peace agreement, knowing well that Syria had just purchased a 27-MW reactor from North Korea. A few weeks earlier, in probably the most damaging article to the Rabin government, the magazine revealed that Foreign Minister Shimon Peres had offered the Vatican hegemony over the Old City of Jerusalem.

Next on the chopping block will likely be *Davar,* the Hista-
drut-owned paper. Its main crime was supporting the wrong candidate for the last Histadrut elections.

What is left are Nimrodi's *Maariv, Yediot Achronot* of the Moses
family, and *Haaretz,* owned by Amos Shocken. *Haaretz* is Labor's
outlet and will not oppose the government for ideological reasons.

Yediot Achronot's intelligence ties to Shimon Peres date from
at least 1984 when Noah Moses had Peres appoint his son-in-law,
the late Amiram Nir, as the prime minister's advisor on counterterrorism. From that position Nir became deeply involved in the
Iran-Contra affair. From the early days of the current government,
Eitan Haber, one of Rabin's most trusted aides, worked in the
Prime Minister's Office while still on salary from *Yediot Achronot.*

Yaacov Nimrodi, another Iran-Contra middleman, worked
with then-defense minister Yitzhak Rabin in arranging the sale of
Israeli arms to Iran. His son Ofer, publisher of *Maariv,* is currently
being investigated for putting listening devices on the phones of
hundreds of the country's political and business leaders. As media analyst Dan Caspi notes, "*Maariv* is not going to go against
Rabin when he is the only thing standing between Ofer and im-
prisonment."

Rabin has used his ties not just to shut down Israel's free press
but its television news as well. Moti Kirschenbaum, Labor's appointee to run the government television station, has so politicized the news that it has lost 80 percent of its viewers in a year.
In a country where over 85 percent of the adult population used
to tune into the news every evening, less than 25 percent do so
today. As one broadcaster told the Jerusalem weekly *Kol Hair,* "We
were recruited to sell peace and reflect the government's policy
only."

On an occasion last April when the evening news covered an
antigovernment demonstration, Rabin had his wife call
Kirschenbaum to warn him that "Yitzhak is really angry." Two
weeks later Kirschenbaum presented a ten-minute feature on a

typical day in the prime minister's life that was later called "crude political propaganda" by the press and debated in the Knesset. Even Kirschenbaum admitted it was "too much."

In just one year since the peace process was announced, over half of Israel's independent publications have disappeared, and the remainder know they have to toe the line if they know what's good for them.

Talk of murder was in the air in Israel. The editors never claimed the rumors were true, but insisted that the very fact that such ideas were circulating was significant. As the "peace" process stumbled along, the atmosphere of intrigue and danger increased enormously, culminating a year later in the Rabin assassination.

Rest in Peace Process

In early August, attorney Shmuel Levinson was murdered in his apartment in the well-to-do Jerusalem neighborhood of Rehavia by, according to police, burglars. An officer at the scene estimated that Levinson must have put up a fierce struggle, and it would have taken two or three men to subdue him long enough to stab him to death.

The month before, state comptroller Miriam Ben Porat had exonerated Police Minister Moshe Shachal of charges that he ordered Yaacov Terner, former chief of Israel police, to quash the investigation of Interior Minister Arye Deri. Terner hired Levinson to reverse the decision and presented him with documentation proving Shachal's guilt. A week before his murder, Levinson threatened Ben Porat with a suit in the supreme court if she did not review Terner's proof.

Terner was one of the first people to be informed of Levinson's murder. On the evening of the tragedy, he had called Levinson to confirm their appointment for the following morning.

Terner's reaction was quick and public. He said, "It is highly unlikely that men intent on burglary are going to commit a murder. Attorney Levinson was killed because he was representing me." In essence, Terner accused Shachal of murder.

Within a week, the police turned up a suspect, a 25-year-old Arab junkie with a record of petty theft. As his father said, "My son has been on narcotics since he was sixteen, and he was too sick and weak to kill anyone. He is also too sick to defend himself."

Even with a suspect in custody, Levinson's murder is steeped in mystery. He had been called by the army for a month's reserve duty and, as was his habit, sent his family to relatives while he was away. The day his duty was to begin, it was cancelled and Levinson was left alone in his apartment. The "burglars" managed to kill him without attracting any attention and this indicates to Terner that the intruders were trained killers.

Had Levinson succeeded in exposing Shachal and Ben Porat, the government would have faced an enormous crisis incriminating its police minister and the supportive Shas Party. Yet Levinson's death is but one in a long list of mysterious demises connected to the peace process.

It is an open secret among the Israeli and foreign media that Jorgan Holst (former Norwegian foreign minister and the arbitrator between Israel and the PLO) did not die of natural causes at age fifty-seven. His death is commonly blamed on knowing too much about what was agreed to at Oslo.

Mordechai Nesiyahu, the director of Beit Beryl, the Labor Party publishing house, also knew a great deal. According to his information, Shimon Peres had no knowledge of the Oslo negotiations and has totally falsified his role in the peace process. A week before his revisionist history of the Oslo agreement was to be published, his 30-year-old son died. According to his son's girlfriend who witnessed the loss, "He was sitting with me and then he just keeled over dead. His heart just stopped."

While Peres' first loyalty was to the European branch of the globalist insiders, the editors discovered that Kissinger was now in the picture.

About the time this article appeared, the Aron/Loftus book The Secret War Against the Jews *was published by St. Martin's Press of New York. The authors convincingly asserted that prior to the U.N. vote on Israel's independence in 1948, David Ben Gurion blackmailed Nelson Rockefeller, threatening to expose Rockefeller's ties to the Nazis during World War II and after unless the dynasty used its influence to sway Latin America to vote in favor of the founding of Israel. Nelson Rockefeller agreed on the condition that Israel neither prosecute nor demand prosecution of Nazi war criminals. That explains why Israel has only tried two war criminals, one unsuccessfully, in forty-eight years. Ben Gurion agreed, Rockefeller lifted his phone, and within hours thirteen Latin American nations switched their votes, tipping the General Assembly vote in favor of Israeli statehood.*

Over four decades later, Ben Gurion's close aide Peres was meeting Rockefeller's employee Kissinger and running off to Latin America on some devious assignment.

Peres Tangos to a Latin Tune

Last June, Shimon Peres met with Henry Kissinger in New York for six hours before embarking on a tour of South America. The aftershocks of the tour were felt a month later when Bolivia begged the Foreign Ministry not to close its embassy in La Paz. In return for keeping it open, Bolivia was prepared to move its embassy to Jerusalem.

The Foreign Ministry turned the offer down, explaining: "Within two years the issue of Jerusalem will be settled and all the embassies will move there anyway." A revealing statement in its own right.

What was never revealed was what the Bolivians were so anxious about in the first place. The Foreign Ministry explained that as a cost-cutting measure Israel would be closing down a number of embassies in Latin America and indeed, following Bolivia, several other countries including Peru and the Dominican Republic also offered to move their embassies to Jerusalem if Israel kept its embassy open in their capitals.

There is no easy explanation for the Latin American desperation to keep their Israeli embassies, but it most likely has a great deal to do with the assignment Kissinger gave Peres last June.

With extensive knowledge of Israel's centralized and corrupt economic system, Inside Israel *was the first publication to point out how expensive and harmful the $10 billion in U.S. loan guarantees really were. As far back as February 1993 it warned that the loan money would be wasted and the Israeli people would be saddled with $10 billion more in debt. By early January 1995 the editors finally realized why the loan guarantees were so important to the Labor government.*

Buying the People

The Ministry of Finance has submitted a request to the U.S. Congress to increase the percentage of the $2 billion in U.S. loan guarantees to be used for budget deficit reduction from $600 million to $900 million.

Although nearly $4 billion in guarantees has been taken by the Israeli government since Rabin took office, Russian activists complain that little of that money has found its way to creating employment opportunities for new immigrants as was its original intention.

In fact, the government has been funneling the majority of the money into the country's major banks, which in turn have been offering easier credit terms for Israelis purchasing new cars and apartments. Since the Rabin government came to power there has been an unprecedented boom in consumer spending fueled by the banks' easier credit lending policies, which a number of economists say is the real reason behind the Rabin government's continuing utilization of the monies from the loan guarantees despite their very high cost and burdensome payback terms.

Selected items from January 1995 amply demonstrate that the IDF's slip from grace had turned into a free-fall, the Vatican was increasing its activities in Jerusalem, Meshulum was continuing to haunt the regime, and everything could be blamed on the all-purpose bugaboo, Iran.

Vatican Update

The Vatican is in the midst of a building program in Jerusalem in anticipation of the year 2000. The program so far includes re-claiming the properties of Notre Dame School (across from the New Gate of the Old City) and Terra Sancta (an educational insti-tute in West Jerusalem) from their Jewish tenants. While Notre Dame is now free of its former residents and is undergoing a major refurbishment, Terra Sancta is proving more troublesome. The tenant, the Hebrew University Biology Department, has been rent-ing most of the building for decades and is reluctant to leave.

Boris Yeltsin meanwhile will not give up Jerusalem without a fight. He ordered his special envoy to Israel to warn Deputy For-eign Minister Yossi Beilin that "the Russian Orthodox Church has more property than the Vatican in Jerusalem, and we want a big say in how the city is to be divided."

Beilin and his Vatican connections are showing up in the strangest places. Likud MK Shalom Silvan informed the Knesset that he is in possession of documents proving that Shmuel Hadas, the former ambassador to Spain, acted as an arbitrator between the Spanish government and the Basque terror organization, ETA, and that Israel's role as a middleman is continuing through Hadas, who was recently named Israel's first ambassador to the Vatican.

Beilin replied to Silvan that he was not aware of Israel's arbitration in the Basque dispute, though he admitted "Israel did serve the same function recently in Guatemala."

IDF Under the Gun

Seldom has the IDF been under more criticism from within than during this past summer. The assaults have come from all quarters and include:

- A "high ranking officer" quoted in *Haaretz* who noted that the new IDF personnel program calls for the hiring of hundreds of new officers in 1995. Yet because the mandate for the last program, which calls for mass firings, has not ended, hundreds of officers are being released. The officer said, "The IDF is acting like a fool."
- A report by the Gush Katif Council claiming that dozens of border guards, both officers and enlisted men, have requested transfers from shared patrols with Palestinian policemen. Citing numerous attacks against them which went unpunished by the police, the soldiers feel "it is humiliating for the IDF to continue the patrols."
- It is well known that the IDF is deliberately not reporting casualties near the autonomous entities for fear of a public backlash. On August 18, six soldiers were injured when their vehicle overturned. The IDF reported that the soldiers were involved in a traffic accident. The soldiers rebelled the next day and revealed that they were deliberately cut off and forced over a drop-off by a Mercedes taxi with Gaza plates.
- MK Ron Nachman is threatening to sue General Ilan Biran, commander of Central Forces, for his orders to reduce significantly the IDF presence in the West Bank to the point of endangering Jewish life. Nachman claims to have documents proving that violent attacks have increased substantially as a result of the troop reduction and that the IDF have stopped reporting the incidents.

- A devastating analysis of the Defense Ministry written by long-time security analyst Reuven Padhatzur and published in the weekly paper *Shishi* accusing Defense Minister Rabin of "letting his ministry fall to pieces."

According to Padhatzur, Rabin has totally neutralized Deputy Defense Minister Motta Gur and leaves the running of the ministry to its director general, David Ivri. The trouble is, Ivri is too busy acting as chief negotiator for military affairs in the peace talks to run his office. Further, he and IDF chief-of-staff Ehud Barak despise each other and can agree on little. Rabin is seldom available to intervene in their disputes; thus, major issues are left unsettled.

Padhatzur adds that Rabin has stripped long term civilian bureaucrats of all power and has no advisers guiding him on policy. Once a week he meets with his favorite generals, most of whom are ex-kibbutzniks like himself, and throws out his ideas. The fawning generals then rubber stamp them into IDF policy. The result is that the country has no long term defense strategy.

- Despite a career as chief-of-staff marred by deadly snafus and cover-ups, Ehud Barak is planning a post-military political career that he hopes will land him in the Prime Minister's Office. Former Labor Party chairman Nissim Zvilli says he will back Barak's bid for power, and during a recent Washington trip Barak met with millionaires Larry Tisch and Edgar Bronfman in order to raise the capital needed to finance his upcoming new career.

Leave the Iranians Out of It

As much as Israel tried to blame Iran for the Buenos Aires blast which killed ninety-five Jews last summer, her plans did not quite work out. Israel is well aware that the true perpetrator of the explosion was Syria, but is covering for her lest an angry public demand an end to their government's desperate quest for a peace agreement between the two countries.

At first Argentina played along and arrested a few Iranian embassy officials, but released them soon after, explaining that it had received "faulty intelligence from the Mossad."

The official Iranian reaction to the arrests was that Argentina "was yielding to pressure from Israel and the U.S. to pin the blame on Teheran for the deadly bombing of the Jewish community center in Buenos Aires." By late August, the state prosecutor of Argentina agreed and handed the Iranian file back to the Justice Ministry noting, "There wasn't a shred of evidence against Iran presented."

Jerusalem's efforts aimed at deflecting the blame from Syria included a disinformation campaign prior to the arrest of the arch terrorist Carlos, claiming that he planned the attack from Beirut. It remains to be seen whether the families of the bomb victims will recover from their shock and demand that the true killers— Hizbollah terrorists under order from Syria and protected by Argentinian president Carlos Menem—face justice.

It is also doubtful if the families of the twenty-three fatalities of the October 17 Tel Aviv bus bombing will ever know that Syria was responsible for the outrage. The first announcement of responsibility for the explosion was relayed from Syrian-controlled Lebanon.

Shortly afterward a Palestinian radio station based in Syria gave details of the attack's methodology a full day before Israeli police pieced together the same conclusions. The attack came two days after Israel and Jordan initialed a peace treaty and some twelve hours after a speech in Cairo by the Syrian president Hafez el Assad condemning the agreement and warning that Syria will embark on a regional destabilization program.

February 1995

As opposition to the Rabin government peaked in early 1995, Inside

Israel's influence was growing in every direction. Intelligence reports
were quoting it, and unknown admirers were reprinting articles from
it on the Internet. Slowly but surely it was becoming the only honest
testament of the current historical record of what was being done to
Israel. It was: "The Betrayal of Israel."

The Brothers in Robes Arrange a Treaty

King Hussein of Jordan is the last line of defense for the Israeli
government. Immediately after each outrage that threatens the
honest testament of the "peace" process, Hussin bails out Rabin.

The day of the killing of kidnapped soldier Nachshon
Wachsman could have been Rabin's swan song. Without consulting his cabinet, Rabin ordered a rescue operation that was a fiasco from its inception to tragic conclusion. Two days later he
and his foreign minister, Shimon Peres, were in Amman celebrat-
ing a diplomatic breakthrough with King Hussein. Talks with the
Jordanians were not scheduled for another month and a half, but
the surprise meeting served the purpose of deflecting blame from
the Wachsman debacle.

Six days later, twenty-three Israelis were slaughtered in Tel Aviv
by a Palestinian bomber. The next day Rabin and Peres initialled
their peace treaty with Jordan, and American President Bill Clinton decided to come to the region to preside over the historic
signing. The Israeli government once again escaped having to face
public wrath over an atrocity.

The treaty was far from uncontroversial yet it was a *fait accom-*
pli before the public had time to consider its consequences. Israel
agreed to give at least 100 million cubic meters of water from the
Sea of Galilee, some 10 percent of its annual supply, to Jordan in
perpetuity. The cost to the country within a decade will be in the
billions of dollars. There was no national debate on why Jordan
had a right to the water or what Israel received in return for its
cost.

President Clinton's visit was stage-managed to the last detail.

To prevent unsightly demonstrations Jerusalem became an armed camp with police gathered in force, streets blocked, and the city closed to vehicles from the territories. The Rabin-Clinton "open" press conference was anything but, as questions were submitted ahead of time by journalists chosen to ask them.

The cooperation between Rabin, Hussein, and Clinton to save the failing Israel/PLO accord is based on more than good will. After Clinton left the country, the president of the Israel Order of Masons placed ads in the major newspapers hailing the trio as "Masons of Peace."

Rabin was inducted into the Masons in 1968, just prior to receiving the post as ambassador to Washington. Though he claims he entered the order innocently and had no later connection to it, in 1976 he presided over an international Masonic convention in Jerusalem.

Masonic handshake of Yitzhak Rabin and King Hussein of Jordan, Nov. 1995

King Hussein is an openly proud high-degree Mason who attends Masonic functions in London several times a year. The peace process was initiated in London under American auspices in November 1992 and since then has been where Israeli leaders including Rabin, Peres, and Likud-head Binyamin Netanyahu, are found whenever momentous decisions are to be made. Rabin rushed to London immediately after initialling the peace agreement with Hussein.

The Masonic plan for the region is a well-kept secret, but Jerusalem is known to be especially important for the organization, as it traces its origins to the mythical Hiram, the mason wrongly believed to have been the planner of Solomon's Temple.

Next African Disaster

In the past year, the Foreign Ministry has established a disturbing pattern. Peace activist Abie Nathan would fly to an African country in distress. He would return to Israel and report to Deputy Foreign Minister Yossi Beilin. Beilin would then send troops to the country to oversee a humanitarian mission. Through circumstances beyond the soldiers' control, the country would descend into chaos.

The pattern was established in Somalia, then Rwanda. In November a new victim was added to the list, namely Zanzibar. This time after Nathan's visit, the Foreign Ministry approved a humanitarian mission to fight malaria.

Africa is not the only continent Beilin has his eye on. First he ordered Israeli police forces to Haiti. After this, the deputy minister of Ireland, Noel Dempsey, flew to Israel to meet him. Their discussions purportedly concentrated on Ireland's participation in the as of yet unofficial U.N. force for "keeping peace" in the Middle East. In return for Ireland's cooperation Beilin offered "improved relations with Israel."

The editors ask, "Who really is Teddy Kollek? Who is he answering to?"

Kollek's Days Aren't Done

In November David Rockefeller visited Jerusalem (his first trip in over a decade), met with Teddy Kollek, and left within a day. Rockefeller's ties to Israel are considered suspicious among many observers who view his guardianship of the Council on Foreign Relations with some trepidation. Among members of this forum who have pushed Israel to make unrealistic security concessions are Secretaries of State Brezinski, Baker, and Christopher.

Officially the reason for Rockefeller's visit was said to be connected to the possibility of setting up a Chase Manhattan branch in Israel, hardly the domain of his longtime friend Kollek.

Though he suffered a humiliating ouster from power in October of last year, Kollek still attracts a great deal of respect outside of Israel. A week after Rockefeller's visit, Kollek was in Cairo for the first time ever and presented Foreign Minister Omar Moussa with a plan for dividing Jerusalem into quarters. The plan, called Metropolitan Jerusalem, was created by the semi-secret Jerusalem Forum, and for some reason was offered to Moussa for Egyptian government approval.

Clinton's Bribe Fails

When President Clinton flew from Israel to Syria, he brought a plan with him. Well aware that the world was watching, he intended to bring President Assad back to Israel with him in one of the most dramatic television events ever. Such a move, he reasoned, could change the results of the upcoming midterm congressional and senatorial elections.

To persuade the Syrian leader to play along, Clinton made an offer: not only would Israel withdraw from the Golan Heights before the next Israeli elections but when it did, with Rabin's consent, the American government would supply the Syrians with the best weapons in its armory, including fully equipped F-16s. Further, Clinton promised Assad that Israel would reduce the size of its army significantly, a vow Rabin made to the Knesset prior to the President's arrival. For the topping on the cake, Clinton pledged to the Syrians that they could have complete control of Lebanon without Israeli or American interference.

Because of opposition to peace with Israel from within his army and recalling the murder of his peace-leaning son Basam, Assad turned Clinton down. Clinton's trip became no more than a PR exercise and had no effect on the midterm elections.

By the fall of 1996, it was clear to those who voted for Netanyahu that he was not fulfilling his campaign promises and was actually carrying on the diplomacy of the previous government, albeit with a different style. Nine months before the elections, Inside Israel *was predicting that this would be the case.*

Netanyahu Backs the Accord

One of the questions that confuses observers is why Likud leader Binyamin Netanyahu has provided such ineffective opposition to the peace process. Under his guidance the party has barely made a dent in the government's program and Netanyahu himself refuses to reveal unsavory information about the country's leadership or to organize public demonstrations.

In July, Netanyahu flew to London where he was instructed not to oppose the upcoming deal with Jordan despite its most problematic clauses concerning water and the three hundred square kilometers of land given up by Israel in the Negev Desert. The treaty went through the Knesset without a debate.

In August, informed sources report that Deputy Foreign Minister Yossi Beilin arranged a meeting between Netanyahu and two financiers, Marc Rich and Pinchas Green, in Geneva. Both are wanted by the FBI for tax evasion. The understanding reached was that if elected in the next elections, Netanyahu would not rescind any clause in the government's accords with the PLO.

As one source in the Foreign Ministry says, "Netanyahu spent five years as the Israeli ambassador to the United Nations. The ties he made there are stronger than his loyalty to the ideals of the Likud." Netanyahu was not the only Likud leader who cut a deal with Jordan in London. According to Yossi Beilin, Yitzhak Shamir sent a personal envoy, Mossad agent Efraim Halevy, to co-sign a tentative peace agreement arranged by Shimon Peres and King Hussein in London and brokered by the U.S. in April 1987.

April 1995

Peres' latest actions confounded the editors as the headline asks. . .

What Is Peres Up To?

Foreign Minister Peres is conducting a very strange national diplomacy and observers are wondering if there is method in the madness. Examples of his peculiar approach abound:

- Peres proposed to U.N. secretary-general Boutros-Boutros Ghali that U.N. troops in Israel and Lebanon be reduced significantly and that the savings to the organization be transferred to the Palestinian Authority in Gaza.
- Peres promised Slovenia's defense minister that Israel would work toward ending the U.N. arms embargo against the breakaway state.
- In a uniquely self-destructive request, Peres pressed the European Union to support a U.N. resolution submitted by the PLO to recognize the rights of Palestinians to self-determination, but

then announced that under no circumstances would the Palestinians ever be allowed a parliament or any other expression of nationhood.

- In one of his wackier but more revealing moments, according to the reliable London-based newspaper *A-Shaark Al-Awst*, just previous to signing the peace treaty with Jordan, Peres tried to meet in Paris with high Syrian officials to present his plan for an Israeli-Jordanian confederation which would share sovereignty over both countries and thus solve the Palestinian-Israeli issue. According to the newspaper, Syria was furious at the proposal and considered such a confederation a dire threat to her security.
- Not satisfied with uniting just two nations, Peres has been the driving force behind a two-part plan to create a united Middle East defense committee which will then join the Security Committee of the European Union.

Superficially, these policies seem contradictory, but in fact a common thread runs through them. The ultimate goal of Peres' diplomacy is to strip Israel of its uniqueness as a nation and meld it into a world family of united states. To this end he is prepared to strip Israel of its sovereignty over its own land in order to share rule with the Hashemite kingdom. And for this reason he is prepared to grant the Palestinians nationhood without a parliament, to make alliances with pariah nations, and to utilize the U.N. to further his aims.

June 1995

In March 1995 one of Inside Israel's *subscribers informed Barry Chamish that he was a longtime friend of Oslo negotiator Ron Pundak and could arrange an interview. Naturally Chamish accepted the opportunity to meet the rather reclusive amateur diplomat. While the editors were waiting for him at a Tel Aviv cafe, Chamish, who*

*had never seen Pundak, predicted that he would arrive wearing jeans,
a vest, and wire-frame glasses, the marching uniform of the Israeli
left. The editors shared a laugh when Pundak arrived in precisely the
garb described.*

*His opinions were just as predictable. For over two hours Pundak
spoke freely about the secret negotiations. Clearly, he felt comfortable
with two secular, educated Jews and believed they shared an
admiration for his accomplishments.*

Pundak confirmed a number of Inside Israel's *prior contentions.
As reported in the newsletter, the official story that all of Washington,
including President Clinton, was delighted to discover for the first
time, in August 1993, that Israel and the PLO had been meeting
secretly since January was a total lie. Pundak reported that his mission
was monitored by the State Department from day one.*

*Second, he confirmed that Peres had nothing to do with the
Oslo negotiations. Only Rabin and Beilin were aware of them until
March of 1993. Peres was lying when he claimed to be an architect
of the talks. And he certainly had* Inside Israel *fooled at first.*

*Finally, he proudly proclaimed that his friend and mentor, Yossi
Beilin, didn't give a fig for national boundaries, believing instead in
one world without borders.*

*Though not realizing the full significance of the Pundak interview,
the editors had indeed collected high level intelligence from well inside
the "peace" process.*

*The June 1995 issue began not with the Pundak interview, but
rather with triumphant confirmation that the newsletter's previous
claim that Peres had sold out Jerusalem to the Vatican was proven
independently.*

Oslo Negotiator Spills Some Beans

In an exclusive interview with *Inside Israel*, Ron Pundak, one of
the two negotiators of the Oslo agreement, inadvertently revealed
a number of important secret facts of the peace process.

For instance, despite Washington's supposed shock at the announcement of the negotiations in August of 1993, the State Department was in on the process from day one. Pundak says he phoned the State Department at the conclusion of each session. Further, Secretary of State Warren Christopher "was very skeptical at the beginning."

Also, Yoel Zinger, a Washington lawyer who had emigrated from Israel fourteen years before, was brought into the process in March. This is very similar to the appointment of Yaacov Frenkel as head of the Bank of Israel. He was a high ranking functionary at the World Bank who was forced on Israel to keep her economy in line with World Bank practices. Zinger, too, was recruited to formulate an agreement to suit Washington's plans.

Pundak admitted that his boss, Yossi Beilin, believes "that national borders are the cause of all conflicts and doesn't view Israel's boundaries as sacred."

Selling Jerusalem to the Ruskies

More proof of the Foreign Ministry's plan to catholicize Jerusalem was revealed in April. Radio Seven, the antigovernment/national religious station broadcast that it had documented proof that in September of 1993 Peres offered hegemony of the Old City of Jerusalem to the Vatican. It claimed to have a copy of a message sent by the Israeli Embassy in Rome to the Foreign Ministry which states: "According to the Peres plan, the Old City will be under the control of the Holy See. This will permit Israel to strengthen its ties to the Catholic world."

Haaretz printed the cable on its front page and, of course, Peres declared that it was a fake. However, he did ask Communications Minister Shulamit Aloni to shut down the radio station.

The Russian Orthodox church is most unhappy with the giveaway to the Vatican, and when the Russian foreign minister visited Israel, he pointedly cancelled a meeting with Yossi Beilin.

Within a few days, Beilin announced that negotiations with
the Russian Orthodox church over land claims in Jerusalem had
been settled and ownership of prime real estate in Jerusalem would
revert to the church. Among the lands now owned by the church
are a large percentage of the property housing the Jerusalem Court
Building and police headquarters.

Who Managed Lebanon's Civil War?

No less than Israel Radio confirmed one of *Inside Israel's* most
conspiratorial claims: that Rabin, Kissinger, and Assad had ignited
the Lebanese Civil War. A report on Israel Radio in late March
says that it received documentation proving the Lebanese Civil
War was manipulated by Rabin, Assad, and King Hussein. The
document referred to is a letter sent from King Hussein to Rabin
in 1974 encouraging a war to wipe out his PLO enemies who had
recently found shelter in Lebanon. Until now, Arab journalists
assumed that in 1974 Kissinger, Rabin, and Assad had agreed to
foment the war. This is the first public claim that Hussein was a
co-conspirator.

For revisionist history buffs, the real reason Menachem Begin
attacked Lebanon in 1982 was to roll back the international
powerbrokers' plans. Begin's minister of defense, Ariel Sharon,
was Prime Minister Rabin's chief antiterrorism advisor, but quit
in 1974 over "Rabin and Kissinger's Lebanon agreement." No one
knew what he meant at the time.

*By mid 1995 the editors were watching Yossi Beilin's every move.
They were convinced that his power derived from his ties (i.e.,
allegiance) to Kissinger and his support of the creation of a world
government run from the United Nations.*

Beilin to Spread His Wings

In Austria, mischievous Deputy Foreign Minister Beilin let another cat out of the bag. He declared that so long as Israel's northern borders were safe, he wouldn't care if Syria took over all of Lebanon. The statement did not bring joy to the soldiers of the SLA, who would be slaughtered if Beilin got his wish.

If Yossi Beilin is having trouble getting rid of the Golan Heights, at least he finally dumped the pesky habit of having foreign dignitaries visit them. For the past two decades, important visitors were taken by the Foreign Ministry to see the Heights first-hand to better understand Israel's security dilemmas. Those days are over. Beilin fought his way through the bureaucracy to have the Golan removed from all future schedules.

Meanwhile, Beilin is expanding Israel's services in Africa. In February he sent a contingent of Israeli firefighters to Somalia to set up two stations in the country's capital. In April he sent a fact-finding commission to Rwanda to see how Israel could be of help to that troubled country. Undoubtedly the visitors will be keeping a close eye out for fire hazards.

August 1995

> *To this day, the editors debate whether Binyamin Ben Eliezer really tried to torpedo the dastardly plans of Rabin and Peres for Jerusalem. His subsequent behavior as a leading advocate of the "peace" process seemed to negate the information received by July of 1995.*
>
> *However, a leading reporter for a mass circulation newspaper told the editors that Ben Eliezer was covertly working against the party leadership and was the source of many leaks. And his comments in Washington did reveal a very different point of view than that he was espousing publicly in Israel.*

Though his later actions against opponents of Oslo seem to defy
the following report, the editors still give him the benefit of the doubt
that he momentarily did try to halt the madness.

A Good Guy in the Cabinet Fails to Save Jerusalem

Housing Minister Binyamin Ben Eliezer has become a fifth column in the Rabin cabinet. In early March he flew to Washington where he declared publicly that Israel's security "had sunk to nothing."

This statement was appreciated by high ranking AIPAC officials, who invited Ben Eliezer to a strategy session. Both sides agreed to coordinate a plan to bring Jerusalem to the top of the negotiating agenda and hopefully torpedo further talks with the PLO.

In May the two-pronged attack was initiated. Ben Eliezer's ministry approved the expropriation of 113 acres of real estate in Jerusalem for construction of housing, largely for the city's burgeoning haredi population. At the same time, AIPAC pressed Senator Robert Dole to lead a campaign to move the American Embassy to Jerusalem.

The double blows initially served their purpose of generating an issue that almost brought down the flimsy peace process, but as should have been expected, the Rabin government caved in to Arab pressure and "froze," really cancelled, the Jewish housing project.

As expected, there was far more to the incident than the Israeli public ever learned. When the expropriations were presented for cabinet approval, most unexpectedly, the princes of appeasement, Foreign Minister Peres and his deputy Yossi Beilin, voted in favor. Their reasoning was influenced by the fact that the expropriated land straddled the Catholic monastery/listening post at Mars Elias near Bethlehem, which the Vatican wants protected against the PLO.

The real war being fought over Jerusalem centers on the year 2000. The foreign participants in the battle, including the Vatican, the Russian Orthodox church, and the Masons, are staking their claims on the city before the end of the millennium. It is essential for the credibility of all three that their tenets and prophecies are achieved and Israel be caught in an Armageddon situation. If the year 2000 passes without judgment in Israel, believers will abandon the churches by the droves, while the Masonic program for chaos followed by a one-world government will have to be put on ice, perhaps for centuries.

The few analysts who are following the events have reached the conclusion that Rabin and Kings Hussein of Jordan and Hassan of Morocco are representing the Masonic interests, and Peres and Beilin are in the midst of a balancing act with the Vatican and the Russian Orthodox church. As has been reported by numerous sources, Peres promised the pope hegemony over the Old City in March of 1993, while in May of this year Beilin handed the Russians title over disputed land in the heart of downtown western Jerusalem.

After the expropriations were announced, Hassan and Hussein sent a joint declaration to Rabin promising to cut all relations with Israel if the government went through with its plan.

There are two other actors in the drama: the PLO and the religious Jewish constituency of Israel, but especially of Jerusalem. Reports of Peres' secret accords with the Vatican began appearing in the Jewish religious community in March, forcing Peres to cover up his perfidy. This he has not done so skillfully.

In March, the Arutz Sheva radio station received a copy of a cable from the Israeli Embassy in Rome to the Foreign Ministry in Jerusalem outlining Peres's deal with the Holy See. The Ministry admitted the cable was genuine, but that it had been tampered with. The word "not" had supposedly been whited out; the true message was that Peres would not hand control of the city to the pope. Incredibly, haredi rabbis accepted this explanation and let Peres off the hook. But he did get a taste of their anger and understood that they do pose an existential threat to his plans.

One side effect of the expropriations was to ease haredi neighborhood crowding and thus deflate religious anger. In a desperate search for housing, the haredim bribed numerous contractors in the city of Bet Shemesh, between Jerusalem and Tel Aviv, to build them new neighborhoods. Under pressure from the city leadership, Ben Eliezer forced contractors to sign an agreement not to construct haredi housing and thus utterly change the character of the city.

By doing so, Ben Eliezer left the government little choice but to find new land for the haredim within Jerusalem. After freezing the expropriations, Rabin ordered Ben Eliezer to rescind his ban on building haredi neighborhoods in Bet Shemesh.

The Palestinian leadership is completely aware of the Israeli government's "Armageddon Plan" for Jerusalem, and PLO chief Yasser Arafat has been trying to short circuit them.

In the midst of the expropriation controversy in early June, two of Israel's most respected journalists, Nahum Barnea and Shimon Shiffer, published a remarkable story in *Yediot Achronot.* According to the two columnists, early in the "peace" process Arafat demanded total control of East Jerusalem for himself. This raised the fury of Kings Hussein and Hassan and they contacted Rabin, who was equally furious.

A meeting subsequently took place in Rabat, Morocco, between King Hassan and a few trusted aides, Rabin representatives Jacques Neria and Rafi Edri, and PLO peace negotiator Abu Mazin. According to Shiffer and Barnea:

> The participants discussed the central question of how to get rid of Yasser Arafat. Among the ways discussed was to have him killed.

Israel TV contacted Neria, Edri, and Abu Mazin for reactions, and while all denied the story, they did not do so convincingly. Neria, for instance, said the revelation could cost him his life.

Since that life-threatening incident, Arafat has taken a different strategy. In blatant contravention of the Oslo accords, he is
running a very active religious ministry in Jerusalem headed by
Khasan Tahabob. His authority extends even to issuing Jerusalem
citizenship papers. The ministry's target is no less Jordan than
Israel, as Mahmoud Abu Eid, a Palestinian journalist working for
a London-based, Saudi-financed newspaper, explains in a private
interview:

> The Palestinians are opposed to the Israeli peace treaty with
> Jordan because of secret clauses that give King Hussein control
> over the Holy Places of Islam. Hussein's Masonic ties are well
> known to Arab reporters, and we believe Hussein is being used
> to give his friends in London a foothold in the city by the year
> 2000. The Palestinians, meanwhile, have been left out.

The plans of Ben Eliezer and AIPAC were supposed to throw a
spanner in the works, but everyone underestimated the
government's capability for retreat. The first step taken was a
disinformation campaign aimed at convincing the angered parties and the Israeli public that the expropriations were the work
of a small cadre of civil servants within the Housing Ministry who,
following bureaucratic orders, put into action a housing plan
approved by the Shamir government. Missing in this explanation
was Ben Eliezer and the cabinet's approval of the program.

When the "we made a mistake" strategy failed to pan out,
Peres and Rabin agreed to freeze the expropriations and let the
actors play out their roles in the Armageddon Plan

Chapter 7

September 1995

> *The editors of* Inside Israel *took their riskiest stand yet when they decided to run a story exposing the deep contradictions in the suicide of Rabin's deputy defense minister, Motta Gur. Gur was found dead at 8:45 in the morning; he was buried by 5:00 in the afternoon. This was not the way prominent Israelis were honored. He was shot in the neck, hardly the usual target for suicide, and he left a one-line note saying he didn't want his family to suffer anymore. This was in reference to his terminal cancer.*
>
> *The problem was, his doctor said he no longer had terminal cancer. There was, thus, no reason for his suicide. But as an insider who more and more openly opposed Rabin's "peace" process, especially the military side of it, there was a strong motive for murder.*

The Murder of Motta Gur

Deputy Defense Minister Motta Gur was found shot dead outside his home on a warm July morning, and was buried just eight hours later. There had been no autopsy, and the funeral took place with unseemly haste. A very short note was found nearby. In it Gur allegedly wrote that he didn't want his family to suffer.

The story of Gur's terminal cancer was spread quickly through the media, accompanied by photos of him taken at the worst time of the illness. The only problem with the story was that Gur was almost cured of the disease.

According to Prof. Samario Chaitchik, director of the oncology department at Ichilov Hospital where Gur was being treated:

In 1989 Gur was treated and responded well to therapy. However, two years ago he had a relapse and received a new treatment. He responded well and the growth was stopped.

Two months ago we found a brain tumor. Gur was treated at Memorial Hospital in Manhattan. Seven weeks ago he returned to Israel. He was greatly improved and his tumor completely disappeared, as did the side effects of the treatment. We saw him three days ago and he gave no sign of desperation. He never asked how long he had to live and he made an appointment to see us again in ten days.

Gur's tumor had disappeared and he was on the way to a complete recovery. The official explanation for his suicide was, thus, totally flawed.

Other testimony belies the story as well. His aide, Rachel Popovich, was one of a chorus of people who noted, "He never said a thing or gave a hint to me." The evening before his alleged suicide, he promised television reporter Avi Bettelheim that he would sit for an interview with him. "Give me a few more days and it'll be all right," were his last words to him. Family members insisted that he was not a suicidal type.

Among those who mourned him most were the settlers of the West Bank and Gaza. He was their last and only link to the government. As Uri Ariel, chairman of the Yesha Council recalls, "He was the only one in the government who helped us with our security problems. We considered him our friend."

Tzvi Hendl, chairman of the Gush Katif Regional Council adds, "We lost a true friend. He was with us in our worst moments and passed our messages to the government."

Gur's sympathies to the settler cause even led him to visit the Jewish community of Hebron proper. But his most publicized act occurred a month previously when he visited a new and illegal settlement constructed near the West Bank town of Barkan.

Pictures of the event show a healthy man, not the sickly image shown after his demise to corroborate the suicide story. Returning to the Knesset, Gur caused an uproar when, according to

Maariv of June 15, 1995:

> It's not that Gur didn't condemn the settlers but rather came to
> their defense: "I must say I asked myself why we didn't settle
> the place years ago? In 1946 as youths we founded thirteen
> kibbutzim the same way." Gur's pronouncement led to hours
> of vigorous debate which almost resulted in several MKs being
> ejected from the forum.

The announcement of Gur's suicide was met with widespread
skepticism and no end of speculation. The most common theory
was that he objected to Defense Minister Rabin's appointment of
Ehud Barak as interior minister and was going to oppose it. A
second theory was that he was going to finally reveal what he
knew about his boss Rabin's peace process.

What is certain is that when Gur passed on, the last hope of
any reconciliation between the government and settlers went with
him, as did the many secrets held in the Defense Ministry that he
was privy to.

———————————

And now the editors quizzically ask . . .

What Is Hussein Up To?

Binyamin Netanyahu's secret July visit with King Hussein and
Crown Prince Hassan of Jordan in London was his fourth this
year. The Likud chief was reportedly furious when news of his
meeting leaked. The only explanation he offered for the talks were
to discuss "Jordanian governmental problems." He also gave his
blessings to a meeting between Hussein and his Likud rival, David
Levy, the next day in Paris.

Which begs the question of why the king would fly especially
for a meeting with Levy. The monarch has recently organized mys-

terious get-togethers with two other marginal Israeli players: Arye Deri, the accused embezzler of Shas; and Amiram Levine, the IDF chief of Northern Command and the scapegoat for the Tzeelim Bet tragedy.

The editors were privileged to be able to speak with MK Benny Begin in his Knesset office for over an hour. Mr. Begin was reticent, but nonetheless offered some invaluable information.

He is certain that the Oslo Accords were tampered with. He notes that the final draft had unexplained gaps and that the spelling of Palestinians was with a small "p." "Our Foreign Ministry uses the large 'P,'" he explained, "while the Norwegians use the small case spelling. This leads me to believe that our draft was altered before it arrived here."

Mr. Begin displayed a copy of a 1984 document proving Shimon Peres met secretly with the PLO back then. According to Begin, if Peres was caught he said he would use the excuse that he was conducting prisoner exchange discussions.

Most important of all, Mr. Begin confirmed Inside Israel's *contention that Rabin allowed the Syrians to attack Lebanon as part of the disengagement treaty brokered by Henry Kissinger in 1974. "Rabin is proud of what he did and brags about it," he said. "But I think it was immoral."*

November 1995

In May 1996 Chamish asked Netanyahu to comment on his secret meetings in London with the Jordanian royal family and their attorney, Lord Victor Mishcon. He denied that the meetings had taken place, nor did he have any knowledge of Lord Mishcon.

Two weeks later the most uninvestigative newspaper in Israel, the Jerusalem Post, *reported that Netanyahu had conducted six secret meetings in London with the Jordanian monarch over the past two*

*years. This was at least one year before Bibi was elected prime minister.
So why didn't he tell Chamish the truth?*

Binyamin Netanyahu: Non-Leader of the Opposition

Prime Minister Rabin is slipping up and letting some cats out of the bag. Recently he told ABC News that a withdrawal from the Golan Heights wasn't his idea. In fact, George Bush made him support the idea.

Indeed he did. In September 1992 Rabin and Bush met in Kennebunkport, Maine. Bush and his State Department had been responsible for putting Rabin in power and now he was calling in his chips. He wanted Israel out of the Golan Heights and the Administered Territories, and quickly. Rabin was given an ultimatum to prepare the Israeli public for a "painful" Golan withdrawal in exchange for peace with Syria, and was ordered to start talking to the PLO. This was the true beginning of the Oslo Accords. The ties with Kissinger continue to this day. Rabin has met him three times in the past six months including at the U.N.'s fiftieth anniversary celebrations held this past October.

Rabin also let another fact slip out, this time as part of an anecdote in a staged "friendly" interview on Israeli televisions Channel One. It seems Likud chief Binyamin Netanyahu phoned Henry Kissinger and asked him to issue a proclamation against the placement of American troops on the Golan Heights. According to Rabin, Kissinger called him right after to tell him the funny story. As the prime minister tells it, Kissinger told Netanyahu not to bother him with such silly requests any more. The next day, the media carried Netanyahu's version of the story. Yes, he did make a call to Kissinger, but Kissinger was undecided about his position on the Golan Heights issue.

Much has been written about Rabin's ties to Kissinger, the State Department, and ultimately the Council on Foreign Relations. While Rabin was ambassador to Washington from 1968–

72, he fell under Kissinger's spell. Just prior to the outbreak of the Yom Kippur War, Rabin wrote a highly influential article declaring that war in the near future was out of the question. His words effectively created a feeling of apathy within military circles.

During the early days of the Yom Kippur War in 1973, Dr. Kissinger withheld arms from Israel for nine days. According to numerous Arab sources, one of the conditions for rearmament was that after the war Golda Meir resign as prime minister in favor of Rabin. In the wake of the war, now Prime Minister Rabin, Kissinger, and Syrian president Hafez el Assad devised a separation of forces agreement that permitted Syria to annex Lebanon. A civil war was ignited by the plotters to provide a feasible pretext for a Syrian invasion. Rabin began and remained a Kissinger plant in the Israeli government.

In light of Rabin's televised revelation, the public must ask, "et tu, Bibi?" The obvious questions that arise from Rabin's little tidbit are: Why was Netanyahu phoning Kissinger? Who exactly was Kissinger going to issue his proclamation to? Why did he feel impelled to call Rabin to tell him about his conversation with Netanyahu? Why are the leaders of the government and opposition working through Kissinger in the first place?

On the very day Rabin and Arafat signed the Oslo II Accords in Washington, the leaders of Israel's opposition parties gathered in an alternative ceremony where each was to sign an accord denouncing the government's pact. One of the clauses of the alternate accord was a pledge to cancel Oslo II when a new government is formed; this, Netanyahu would not sign. At the last moment he threatened to torpedo the ceremony over the issue of the legitimacy of Oslo II; only when this clause was removed did the signing take place.

It is clear Netanyahu is not leading the opposition. While other MKs have participated in demonstrations, he has stayed home. While backbenchers have tried to expose scandals that in any other democracy would bring down the government, he has refused to support investigations.

Two weeks before the Jordanian peace treaty was completed, Netanyahu was in London meeting with King Hussein. When the treaty with its questionable water and territorial withdrawal clauses was presented to the Knesset, Netanyahu refused to lead a parliamentary debate on the momentous legislation. Instead the public was handed a *fait accompli* without any real understanding of what the government and opposition had agreed to. Shortly after the treaty was signed, Netanyahu was in Amman for a visit. This was followed by at least two more secret meetings with the Jordanian leadership in London.

While Netanyahu conducts secret negotiations with the Hashemite dynasty, something similar is taking place with Syria. Rabin has been publicizing Netanyahu's communications with Assad, which the Likud leader has denied. Unfortunately for him, the Syrian foreign minister confirmed the ties and even President Assad has publicly stated that he can get a better deal from Netanyahu than Rabin.

Rabin's peace process is controlled by outside forces with little regard for the consequences on his own country. Netanyahu's outside ties are no less noteworthy. In the past few months, he has conducted meetings with German chancellor Helmut Kohl, French president Jacques Chirac, British prime minister John Major, and naturally, American president Bill Clinton.

The meeting with Kohl included a state dinner followed by a four-day stay in the country. It is legitimate to ask why the Germans honored the leader of Israel's opposition so royally, and what business he is conducting with the leaders of the West.

Rabin has lately been blaming Netanyahu for inflammatory speeches that have caused violence at demonstrations and made public appearances by the likes of Rabin and Peres nigh impossible in most circumstances. In actual fact, Netanyahu has been pouring water on public outrage and has urged an end to inflammatory language. His actions have assured that the Rabin peace process passes safely through the Knesset, and according to reliable sources he has promised Kohl, Chirac, Major, Clinton, et al, that if the government changes next year, the "peace" process will go on as unhindered as he can arrange.

For this he may have been rewarded. In the past few months Netanyahu has found the funds to purchase a $750,000 apartment in the desirable Jerusalem neighborhood of Rehavia and a $2 million villa in the suburb of Har Adar. Where he found almost $3 million for his upgraded housing standards is a source of legitimate inquiry for his party well before next year's election.

December 1995

The Conspiracy to Murder Yitzhak Rabin

Just previous to the evening of November 4, 1995, Prime Minister Yitzhak Rabin was a very worried man. His peace process with the PLO was not going well with the Israeli public. The latest poll in *Maariv* showed that 78 percent of the public wanted the process stopped until a national referendum was held to decide whether to continue or not. Only 18 percent of Israelis trusted Rabin enough to have him carry on his diplomacy without a public referendum. Rabin couldn't step out in public without being heckled. His most humiliating moment came in August when he was introduced at a soccer game and 40,000 fans jeered him in unison.

But that evening would be different. A coalition of left wing political parties and youth movements had organized a rally in support of him and Rabin knew that, for a change, he would be surrounded by thousands of well wishers.

Which made his murder that evening doubly unexpected. It all seemed so easy. At 9:15 Rabin ad-libbed a speech before 100,000 supporters gathered at a square outside Tel Aviv's city hall. A half hour later, he walked down the steps of the stage into the "sterile" area below where his car awaited him. Here he would be safe from threat because no one but approved security personnel were supposed to be there.

But something was very wrong in the parking lot below. The area, far from being sterile, was crawling with unauthorized personnel. If Rabin had been alert he would have noticed that things were not looking very right at all. First of all, he should have thought, where's the ambulance? There was always an ambulance stationed near his car when he made public appearances, yet this evening it was nowhere to be seen. Then he should have asked, where are the policemen? Dozens of policemen should have been providing security, but only a few were in sight. The parking area was almost totally dark, whereas it was standard security procedure to illuminate his walking route.

But Rabin seemed buoyed by the success of his speech and uncharacteristically walked alone, unaccompanied by his wife, Leah, toward his car. A few seconds before he reached his vehicle, a security agent of the Shabak who was supposed to cover his rear stepped back, stopped, and permitted an assassin, Yigal Amir, to fire three shots.

As soon as the bullets were fired, a Shabak agent yelled, "Srak, srak," or "They're blanks, they're blanks," while another agent told Rabin's wife Leah a few moments later not to worry because "the shots were blanks." The agents next to Rabin pounced on the killer and cuffed him. His first words after being apprehended were, "Why are you handcuffing me? I did my job. Now it is time to do yours." The first question the Shabak agents asked the assassin was, "Didn't you fire blanks?"

Since there was no ambulance, Rabin was rushed to the hospital in his own car. Instead of taking a minute to arrive at the hospital, the 700-meter trip mysteriously took over eight minutes to complete. During this time the driver claimed he "became confused" and got lost. He didn't use his radio, even to report his position or inform the hospital that he was on the way. Thus the hospital staff were totally unprepared to treat Rabin. A few minutes later, dozens of reporters received messages from a spokesman from an unknown group called Jewish Vengeance promising to get Rabin next time. After the announcement of his death, the spokesman called the reporters back to retract the earlier announcement.

At 11:15 p.m., Rabin aide Eitan Haber, holding what he claimed was a bloody song sheet Rabin had sang from at the rally, announced the prime minister's death. That task done, Haber rushed to Jerusalem and cleaned out the files of Rabin's Defense Ministry office. He apparently couldn't wait until the next morning, and later told a reporter from the weekly magazine *Kol Hair* that "I wanted to be sure the files were donated to the archives of the Israel Defense Forces (IDF)."

What Happened to Yigal Amir in Riga?

Accused killer Yigal Amir had served honorably in the elite Golani Brigade of the Israel Defense Forces. Immediately after his release he was sent to Riga, Latvia, in the spring of 1992 on some sort of mission by a covert branch of the Prime Minister's Office, the Liaison Department.

Founded in 1953 to educate and rescue Jews from behind the Iron Curtain, the Liaison Department had become a nest of spies over the years. As the daily newspaper *Haaretz* reported a few weeks after Rabin was killed: "The Liaison Department conducts its own diplomacy and has its own private agenda."

Amir was an activist for reputedly the most radical antigovernment organization of all, Eyal. The head of Eyal, Avishai Raviv, was filmed by Israeli TV a month and a half before leading an induction ceremony in which new members vowed to kill anyone who "sold out the land of Israel." If Eyal was really a secret organization, why did the members allow themselves to be filmed by Israel TV and expose themselves to the public?

A week after Rabin was killed, on November 12, journalist Amnon Abramovich revealed on Israel TV that Eyal was set up by the Shabak to provoke and trap right-wing radicals and its leader, Avishai Raviv, was an agent whose code name was "Champagne," referring to the bubbles of incitement he raised.

Raviv was an agitator on the campus of Bar Ilan University, where Amir studied. He befriended Amir and encouraged him to organize study weekends in Hebron. As it turned out, Raviv was no newcomer to the Shabak. Back in 1987 he was supposed to be expelled from Tel Aviv University for his radical activities by the dean, Itamar Rabinovitch, who until just recently was Rabin's chief negotiator with the Syrians. Then-prime minister Yitzhak Shamir ordered his aide Yossi Achimeir to personally intervene on Raviv's behalf. Thus Raviv was not recruited after Rabin came to power.

Eyal had only two members, Raviv and Erin Agelbo. They shared a rented apartment in the Hebron suburb of Kiryat Arba in the same building where Baruch Goldstein once resided. But Agelbo, it turned out, was not just an ordinary, everyday extremist either. After the weekly magazine *Yerushalayim* printed his picture, a reader recognized him as a Jerusalem policeman who trained her in weapons use during a stint in the civil guard. Lo and behold, a link between the assassination and the police emerged. The Jerusalem police department owned up and admitted Agelbo was a "former policeman who was fired for his radical activities in 1994."

Shortly after the murder, the Israeli media began exposing some very incriminating evidence. The most serious was that Yigal Amir was a Shabak agent. The first to make the accusation publicly was Prof. Michael Hersigor, a left-wing political science professor at Tel Aviv University. On November 11, a week after the killing, he told a reporter from *Yediot Achronot:*

> The murder of the prime minister has no rational explanation. There is no explaining the breakdown and no telling what happened. But in my opinion it would be advisable to seek the connection between Amir and the Shabak. It's possible there was a conspiracy. It turns out the murderer was in the Shabak when he travelled to Riga. He was supplied with false documents with which to receive a gun license. It sounds like he had connections to the Shabak at the time of the murder.

The heat was turned up when Alex Fishman of *Yediot Achronot* reported that Amir was trained by the Shabak in Riga. Soon after, Army Radio broadcasted an interview with Rabbi Benny Elon, a leader of the Jewish settlement movement, who said:

> The Shabak was responsible for the founding and funding of Eyal and its leader Avishai Raviv. I claim that the Shabak knew Eyal's every move before the assassination and that the Shabak funded its activities.

With the facts closing in, the government embarked on a sloppy cover-up of Amir's Riga days. In order: the government press office announced that Amir, who spoke no Latvian and had no teaching credentials, was a Hebrew teacher in Riga for five months. The head of the Liaison Department (whose name was whited-out of a *Maariv* article) then changed the story to read he was a teacher for two to three months. After this, minister of internal security Moshe Shachal told Israel TV that Amir was a security guard in Riga for two months, which was probably the closest version to the truth. Finally, running out of ideas, Aliza Goren, spokesperson for the prime minister, announced in late December that the Prime Minister's Office is now certain Amir was never in Riga and that any journalist writing so "was acting irresponsibly." That ploy fell apart when the BBC filmed a copy of Amir's passport with the letters "CCCP" clearly stamped in it.

But this wasn't the end of the story of the prime minister's strange Liaison Office. In the months prior to the assassination, the State Comptroller's Office initiated an investigation of profound corruption at the Liaison Office and the unexplained disappearance of a great deal of money in the C.I.S. In late 1992, Rabin announced he was considering closing down the Liaison Office for good.

The Kempler Film
A so-called amateur photographer, Ronnie Kempler, filmed the murder of Rabin. He had no camera of his own, so he borrowed

one from his sister and hung around on a balcony overlooking the parking lot for over an hour, unquestioned. He claimed he had "an odd feeling" about Amir and focused in on him for long periods of time.

His film clearly shows Amir signalling someone in the distance a few minutes before the shooting, and it captures the unexplainable decision of Rabin's rear guard to abandon his position and clear the way for Amir. What the tape shows (albeit does not prove) is that Yigal Amir pointed a gun at Yitzhak Rabin and shot at him. But what if the bullets weren't real?

The amateur film of the Rabin assassination has since been examined by numerous people in frame by frame sequence and found to have been sloppily cut and edited. The strangest part of it is Rabin's reaction to being shot. Instead of lurching forward from the bullets, he alertly turns back, seemingly aware of the events taking place.

Kempler works for the State Comptroller's Office. Even the most skeptical Israeli had to ask why the fateful moment wasn't captured on film by a car salesman, postal carrier, or computer programmer. Why was he employed by the very office that was investigating the former employer of the assassin?

At the very moment Rabin was shot, Kempler stopped filming. He told Israel's Channel 2 interviewer Rafi Reshef that it was because "he had seen enough." Yet he told another journalist he had dropped the camera, and another, that a policeman told him to stop shooting. When the beta film was converted for viewing on national television, the technician who did the transcribing claimed that the sound of the agent yelling "blanks, blanks" was removed.

Other than one short appearance on Channel 2 after the film was aired, Ronnie Kempler has never been quoted publicly in any newspaper—anywhere.

The Shamgar Commission
The testimony of policemen at the Shamgar Commission ham-

pered a clean cover-up. While the Shabak chose to exonerate the police of all responsibility for the murder, the chief of the Tel Aviv Police Department, Gabi Lest, testified that his men were supposed to secure the sterile area, but were not stationed by Rabin's security men. Those policemen were shocked to see that the Shabak officers were not in place.

What the policemen testified to compromises the "lone gunman" theory, which the commission personally appointed by Prime Minister Shimon Peres eventually ruled was the case.

Officers Sergei and Boaz testified that they saw Amir talking with a bearded man in a tee shirt that he appeared to know about twenty minutes before the shooting. Sargeant Saar testified that he saw Amir's brother Hagai, who was later charged with supplying the bullets for the assassination, near the crime scene shortly before the murder. Officer Sharabi testified that "a man who we knew by face as an anti-Rabin demonstrator rushed at Rabin, shook his hand, and left."

Sergei became suspicious of the whole atmosphere and specifically of Amir. He asked another officer who Amir was, and was told he was working undercover. The police claimed that Amir got into the sterile area when he presented government credentials given to him by the Liaison Office.

Thus the Shabak allowed Amir, who had been filmed being taken away kicking from a demonstration at Efrat by the Shabak two weeks earlier; another known demonstrator, Amir's brother (supposedly carrying bullets); an unknown film maker; and a mysterious man wearing a tee shirt, to roam at will in an area that was meant to be cordoned off to unauthorized personnel.

Reconstructing the Murder
There are only two explanations for Rabin's assassination. One is that the Shabak, one of the world's most respected security organizations, is incompetent. The other is that agents on the scene allowed the assassination to take place. Probably with Rabin's knowledge, the Shabak set up Amir.

The theme of the gathering on the fateful night was, "No to Violence." Amir was to have shot Rabin with blanks, Rabin was to have miraculously escaped an assassination attempt, and then climbed back on the stage with a stirring speech written by his close aide, Eitan Haber. The public would react with revulsion against the attempted assassination by an extremist right-winger, and the government could justify a crackdown against opponents of the peace process.

What Does Amir Know?

Consider the fate of Yoav Kuriel, a policeman assigned to protect Rabin. Within a week of Rabin's murder, Kuriel was also found dead, though how he died is a mystery since his internal organs were removed purportedly for transplantation. The government claimed he committed suicide and buried him in a closed funeral at Hayarkon Cemetery outside of Tel Aviv. Traffic was diverted for ninety minutes while the funeral took place.

Maariv investigative journalist David Ronen succeeded in tracking down Kuriel's death certificate. The hospital, in a blatant disregard for procedure, left out the reason for death.

One day during his trial Amir screamed to the reporters, "Why don't you print the story about the murdered bodyguard?" He was asked which one. "The one who yelled the bullets are blanks."

And Amir wasn't finished. He added, "I know enough to bring down the whole regime. The whole business has been a charade. The entire system is rotten. I will be forgiven when people know the whole story."

If that outburst was for public consumption, it was certainly consistent with what he has been saying privately. On November 29, 1995, according to a report published by *Maariv* in early January 1996, he complained to the police officer taking testimony, "They're going to kill me in here."

"Nonsense," replied the officer.

"You don't believe me. Well, I'm telling you it was a conspiracy. I didn't know I was going to kill Rabin."

"What do you mean? You pulled the trigger, it's that simple."

"Then why didn't Raviv report me? He knew I was going to do it and he didn't stop me? And why wasn't I shot to save Rabin?"

Who Killed Yitzhak Rabin?

By the early spring of 1996 new evidence led to the proposition that Yigal Amir shot blanks while Rabin was murdered with real bullets inside his car, not by the blanks that Amir fired.

On May 3, 1996, Amir's lawyers filed an appeal to the Supreme Court based in part on a doctor's testimony that Rabin's wounds and burn marks indicated a point-blank shot. However, according to the weekend newspaper of *Maariv, Zman Tel Aviv*, all doctors and staff on duty the night of the Rabin assassination were receiving death threats. The doctor's testimony disappeared from the appeal. Instead, enticing second-hand testimony was presented by a taxi driver who was told by his passenger, an Ichilov Hospital pathologist, that Rabin was shot three times at point-blank and near point-blank ranges.

Amir's lawyers pointed out that the bullets may have been tampered with since there is no record of what happened to them between the time they were removed from Rabin's body on the night of November 4 and the time they were delivered to the Abu Kabir Forensics Institute at midnight on November 5.

Amir's attorneys had indisputable proof that Rabin was shot point-blank and not from the fifty to seventy centimeters claimed by the Shamgar Commission and seen in the Kempler film. Chief Lieutenant Baruch Gladstein of the Israel Police Fibers and Materials Laboratory conducted thorough tests of Rabin's suit and shirt and determined by the size of the bullet holes and the concentration of gunpowder and other particles that Rabin was shot once from less than twenty centimeters distance and once, point-blank. He also concluded that the bullet which shot Yoram Rubin was not of the same composition as the bullets which went through Rabin's clothing.

One of the very first media reports on the murder was an eye-

witness account given to Israel TV by Miriam Oren. She said when
she saw Rabin get into the car "he did not look at all like he was
shot. He climbed in on his own." When Kempler's film begins
again after the shooting, it shows Rabin's car speeding off. Three
seconds before Rabin entered his car, the back passenger door
(Rabin entered the car through the rear driver's side, followed by
Rubin) closes. Someone was already in the car waiting for Rabin
and as the prime minister entered, grabbed the car door and shut
it from the inside.

Amir's appeal was also based on the testimony of dozens of
eyewitnesses who testified that Amir was never close enough to
Rabin to have fired these shots. The eyewitnesses say that the gun-
shots had an odd, distinctive sound, whereas tests of Amir's gun
showed that its sound was perfectly normal. In July, police officer
Yossi Smadja was quoted in *Maariv* as saying that he was almost
next to the assassination site and heard five shots, three clear and
two muffled.

What they heard were the muffled shots of the bullets that
killed Rabin coming from inside the car. Amir told the police
immediately after the event that he had put nine bullets in his
gun. However, eight were found in his clip. Two bullets were un-
accounted for.

Then there is the testimony of Shimon Peres who saw Rabin's
body in the hospital. He claimed in *Yediot Achronot* in late September that Rabin's forehead was swollen and bruised, he thought
from being pushed on the pavement after he was shot. This is in
direct contradiction to the eyewitness report of Miriam Oren who
was beside Rabin after Amir pulled the trigger. She told Israel TV
moments after the incident that Rabin walked into the car under
his own power. Where, and how then, did the bruises that Peres
claims he saw occur?

Finally, there is the indisputable proof offered unintentionally by Rabin's aide, Eitan Haber. While Rabin was being oper-
ated on at Ichilov Hospital, for reasons unexplained to this day,
Haber rifled through his suit and shirt pockets looking for some-

thing and pulled out the song sheet Rabin had held at the rally. Haber produced it at Rabin's funeral, but did not explain why if Rabin was shot in the back, the sheet taken from the chest pocket was so bloody. Nor did he explain why he had the sheet and not the police forensics laboratory.

On September 20, two Israeli newspapers printed interviews with most unexpected subtle advocates of the conspiracy thesis. After nine months of silence Shlomo Levy gave an interview to *Yerushalayim*. Levy was an associate of Amir's who was a soldier in the Intelligence Brigade of the IDF. After hearing Amir's threats to kill Rabin, he reported them to his commander who told him to go to the police. The police took his testimony very seriously on July 6, 1995, and transferred it to the Shabak where it was ignored until three days after the assassination.

The report concludes, "Levy's was only one of a number of reports the Shabak ignored about Amir. . . . The fact that the Shabak let the reports gather dust until Rabin was murdered lends credence to numerous conspiracy theories."

Levy was asked, "If you did the right thing, why have you been hiding in your home out of fear?" He replied, "The Shabak is big and powerful and I'm a little guy. The assassination is an open wound with them and who knows how they'd react if I let myself be interviewed." On the same day, Rabin's son Yuval was interviewed in *Yediot Achronot*. Asked if he believed his father was killed in a conspiracy, a question that said much about the public's interest, he replied, "I can't say yes or no. It's not hard to accept it. . . . One thing is certain, no one was punished. The worst that happened to any Shabak agent was he lost his job."

Considering the evidence, Yitzhak Rabin was not killed by Yigal Amir. It's possible that most of Rabin's security guards and most likely Rabin himself, thought there was going to be an elaborate sting to catch the "right-wing radical" Yigal Amir red-handed. Amir himself may have been drugged or duped into believing that his bullets were real and that he really did kill Rabin. He may have been programmed to take the blame.

Whoever was behind this coup also had the help of the Shamgar Commission whose conclusions merely reinforced the manufactured media image in the Israeli public's mind that radical Jewish extremism was responsible for the murder. The cover-up was as insidious as the crime.

Rabin Murder Cover-Up Goes Public

The month of October 1996 saw the blatant inconsistencies between the official version of events surrounding the Rabin assassination and the truth clash publicly. Early in the month, *Maariv*'s weekend magazine published a remarkable collection of testimony from seven policemen and security agents on duty at the assassination scene.

The *Maariv* report also dealt with the issue of whether the alleged assassin Yigal Amir's bullets were real or not. It is not denied by the Shamgar Commission that, "Blanks, blanks," was yelled by someone while Amir shot his weapon. The conclusion is that Amir yelled it to confuse Rabin's bodyguards, a contention he denies. It turns out that more than just, "Blanks, blanks," was shouted.

S.G.—*Shabak agent under command of Rabin's bodyguard Yoram Rubin:* "I heard very clearly, 'They're not real, they're not real,' during the shooting."

A.A.—*personal security head of the Shabak:* "I heard one shot and someone shouting, 'Not real, not real.' I can't say with certainty if it came from the shooter."

Avi Yahav—*Tel Aviv policeman:* "The shooter yelled, `They're caps, nothing, caps.'"

None of the police or security men heard the famous "Srak, srak," ("blanks, blanks") shout. The scene they describe is of a number of people shouting different phrases. What united the shouters was their belief that blank bullets were being shot.

How Many Bullets Were Shot?

A.H.—*agent assigned to Yoram Rubin's staff:* "I heard one shot, followed by another."

Maariv to A.A.: "Are you certain you only heard one shot?"

A.A.: "Absolutely certain."

Avi Yahav: "I heard a number of shots. I'm not sure how many."

S.G.: "As I approached the car, I heard three shots."

The inability of security and police personnel trained to testify in court to agree on the number of shots is puzzling, but on one issue all agree: none thought Rabin was hurt.

Y.S.—*Shabak head of security for the Tel Aviv rally:* "I heard Rabin was wounded only when I arrived at Ichilov Hospital some minutes later."

S.G.: "I didn't hear any cry of pain from the prime minister and didn't see any signs of blood whatsoever. . . . It wasn't until some time after that I was told that Yoram Rubin was hurt."

A.A.: "Only after a number of inquiries as to whether Rabin was hurt, did I drive in shock to Ichilov."

None of the security or police personnel detected any sign that Rabin was hurt, a quite inexplicable fact when one considers that he was not merely hurt but supposedly shot in the lung and spleen by two hollowpoint 9 mm bullets. However, the "amateur" film of the assassination exonerates the witnesses. After the film shows the blast from Amir's gun, Rabin is not pushed forward by the pressure of the bullet, nor does he evince pain. Rather, he keeps on walking and turns his head quickly to his left.

The *Maariv* article reported that the assassination film shot by Ronni Kempler pointed out that three seconds before Rabin entered his car, the opposite side passenger door is slammed shut. The only way the door could be shut was if someone was inside the car shutting it. This would be in contradiction of the Shamgar report which has Rabin and Rubin entering an empty car.

The *New York Times* of November 8, 1995, quotes Yoram Rubin, Rabin's head of personal security, as saying that Rabin's last words to him in the car were that he was hurt but not seriously. Yet he told the police a different story on the night of the murder and later testified to the Shamgar Commission and at Yigal Amir's trial.

- *Rubin to the police from 1:07 a.m., November 5, 1995:* "I lifted the prime minister and pushed him into the car."
- *To the Shamgar Commission:* "He [Rabin] helped me get up. That is to say, we worked together. . . . We jumped, really jumped. I'm surprised, in retrospect, that a man his age could jump like that."
- *At Amir's trial:* "I grabbed him by his shoulders and asked him, Yitzhak, do you hear me, only me?"

In this version Rabin did not answer at all. In previous versions he said he wasn't hurt badly or actually helped Rubin to his feet.

Perhaps the most confusing piece of testimony concerns the critical moments when he enters the car with Rabin. The assassination film shows the opposite back passenger door being closed from the inside and the other back door being pushed closed from the outside. Yet Rubin testifies: "We fell onto the seat together and I slipped between the front and back seat. His legs and mine were dangling outside as I yelled to the driver, 'Get out of here.' He started driving and I lifted his [Rabin's] and my legs inside and closed the door. This all took two to three seconds."

A most curious incident occurs on the way to Ichilov Hospital, normally less than a minute's drive from the supposed murder site. The trip took from 9:45 to 9:53. With a minute and a half driving time to go, Rabin's driver, Menachem Damti, picks up a policeman, Pinchas Terem, to help direct him to the hospital. Damti, an experienced driver, needed no help in finding Ichilov, but even that isn't the main point. With the prime minister dying beside him, Yoram Rubin says to the new passenger, "I'm wounded. Bandage me."

As for Rabin, we can only guess he didn't care that his wounds needed much more urgent attention. Terem completed his bizarre testimony by noting that Damti did not notify Ichilov by radio that he was coming and thus the hospital staff was totally unprepared for Rabin's arrival.

One conclusion that can be reached from the testimony of all the witnesses is that Rabin was unhurt by Amir's blank bullets and was shot inside the car. Rubin took a harmless arm wound to cover his role in the event and Damti picked up a policeman as a witness in case of future disbelief.

More Questions About the Kempler Film

There are also disturbing questions about the film of the assassination taken by Roni Kempler. The first is, why did Kempler wait a month to show the film when he would have been a few million dollars richer had he sold it to the international media outlets the day following the assassination? In his sole television appearance the night his film was broadcast, he explained he wasn't interested in making money.

No one initially knew that he made the film or that a film of the assassination existed. Does that mean none of the security agents on the scene spotted him filming from a rooftop? How did the video get to the media? Shouldn't the Shabak have confiscated the film if this was the only documentary evidence describing the crime? And why didn't the filmmaker voluntarily turn over the film to the police?

It isn't completely certain even if the film is authentic. In the opinion of many who have seen it, it has been tampered with. The event captured on the film that is the centerpiece of doubt is the issue of the door of Rabin's vehicle that closes before he enters the car. To almost everyone who watches that door close, it is certain that someone, likely the murderer, was waiting in the Cadillac for Rabin. This is in direct contradiction to the Shamgar Commission's conclusion that Rabin entered an empty car followed by his bodyguard, Yoram Rubin, and his driver, Menachem Damti.

What many people find haunting is Shimon Peres' behavior on the film. After greeting the crowd, he walks to Rabin's car with four Shabak agents, stops, looks inside and points to Amir seated nine feet away. At this point there is a cut in the film and we now see Peres conversing with Rabin's driver, Menachem Damti.

Peres enters his car and Rabin descends the steps. The camera captures the agents at Rabin's rear stopping and allowing Amir a clear shot at Rabin. Amir draws his gun from deep inside his pocket and at that point he should have been pounced on. He lifts the gun and shoots. Running the murder frame by frame, Rabin has supposedly taken a hollowpoint 9 mm bullet in his lung, yet he doesn't wince or flinch. He is not even pushed forward by the impact, nor does his suit show signs of tearing. Instead, he continues walking forward and turns his head behind him in the direction of the noise.

Was Rabin's reaction medically feasible? There are two types of pain reaction, one reflexive, the other delayed. Rabin, did not display the reflexive reaction, which would have most likely meant clutching the arm. Instead, he displayed a startle reaction, painlessly turning his head toward the direction of the shot.

Rabin takes two steps forward and suddenly the film becomes totally hazy for a few seconds. Within the haze, two more shots are heard but not seen. It is possible that the film was deliberately made fuzzy by an artificial process duplicating a sudden, quick movement of the camera. A white reflective light on the film stays in the same position while the camera is supposedly jerking. According to the testimony of Rabin's bodyguard Yoram Rubin and of the final conclusion of the Shamgar Commission, the following is what happened:

> After hearing the first shot, Rubin jumps on Rabin and pushes him to the ground. Amir approaches Rabin and Rubin and while being held by other bodyguards pumps one bullet into Rubin's arm and another into Rabin's spleen at 25 cm distance. There is now a hiatus in the shooting and then according to Rubin, "I

said to him, 'Yitzhak, can you hear me, just me?' He [Rabin] helped me to my feet—that is, we worked together. He then jumped into the car. In retrospect, I find it amazing that a man his age could jump like that." (It is amazing that a man his age with bullets in his lung and spleen could jump at all.)

According to the Kempler film, 4.6 seconds pass from the time of the second shot, to when Rabin is lifted or pushed into the car. He could not have waited for a hiatus in the shooting and made his dramatic plea to Rabin in that time. Nor is Rabin filmed jumping into the car. Rubin lied.

The police proved conclusively that Rabin was shot point-blank. Amir never shot point-blank at Rabin. The testimony and behavior of Rabin's bodyguard and driver are, to say the least, inconsistent with the truth. Rabin's driver got lost for eight minutes and the time has never been accounted for. It was during this time that Rabin may have been shot and the fourth person in the car, the hitman, was let out in a predetermined location.

Chapter Eight

January 1996

> *Rabin wasn't buried an hour before it was business as usual. The only difference was Peres was forced to assume the dead prime minister's mantle. Instead of promoting the goals of the European branch of the NWO, he was prevailed upon to act as an agent for London and New York.*

Peres' Inexplicable Cabinet Appointments

Israeli Prime Minister Shimon Peres' appointments of Ehud Barak to the second highest post in the government, foreign minister, and Haim Ramon as interior minister appear inexplicable to most Israelis, but are logical in the context of Yitzhak Rabin's previous secret diplomacy.

Barak was arguably the most incompetent chief-of-staff in IDF history. His tenure was marred by fatal accidents, operational failures, and cover-ups. He began his new career by hushing up an incident involving a base commander (and close friend) who was implicated in the accidental killing of a soldier. Barak used his power to quash a trial of the commander.

Then came two accidents at the Tzeelim training base which resulted in the deaths of ten soldiers. In both cases, no officer was found responsible enough to be imprisoned or decommissioned. But it was the second tragedy, called Tzeelim Bet, that involved Barak in pure scandal.

Barak was in attendance at an exercise in which a rocket exploded, killing five soldiers. His role in the planning of the exercise has never been revealed, but it was obviously central. According to a report in *Yediot Achronot*, Barak witnessed the carnage, but merely stood by rather than helping the wounded. Worse, he flew back to Tel Aviv in his helicopter before any of the wounded were evacuated.

Once he arrived in Tel Aviv, a cover-up aided by Defense Minister Yitzhak Rabin began in earnest. A commission of inquiry was set up headed by General Menachem Eichen, who not coincidentally was in command of the central axis during the Lebanon War. Then-Colonel Barak was one of his deputies.

The central axis was the only command which failed to meet its objectives, yet its deputy commanders Barak and Amiram Mitzneh were promoted by Defense Minister Rabin. When Barak was appointed chief-of-staff, the former military liaison to Washington, General Uzi Lev-Tsur wrote, "The failure of the Lebanon War was the inability of the central force to complete its mission. The eastern and coastal forces attained their goals in days, but the division led by Barak and former commander of Judea and Samaria Amiram Mitzneh failed. Yet these are the officers Rabin chose to lead the IDF in putting down the intifada. I'm very worried about how the IDF will perform in the next war if it is led by Barak."

And well he should have been, for Barak was accused this year of giving the order for the worst incident of the Lebanon War, the ambush at Sultan Yaacov, in which twenty-three soldiers died. No officer was held responsible for the fiasco but more than ten years after it happened, General Avigdor Ben Gal, who was commander of the regional battalion, told Israel Radio that his assistant, Ehud Barak, gave the order to advance into the ambush. His version of events was confirmed by an intelligence officer at the scene, Mickey Shachar.

General Eichen apparently forgave Barak at the time, for no commander was held responsible for the deadly order to advance into the Syrian trap. Eichen returned to form in his Tzeelim Bet inquiry by shifting the blame for the tragedy away from Barak and onto junior officers.

The commission's conclusions did not satisfy the families of the victims or the public and another commission had to be set up. This time Barak offered testimony that totally contradicted his version of events at the Eichen Commission and Colonel Amiram Levine was made the scapegoat for the deed. Not that he was punished. Barak later promoted him to chief of Northern Command where his incompetence is at least partly to blame for the forty-four soldiers and two civilians lost in Hizbollah attacks during the past year.

The second commission did no more to satisfy four of the victims families and they demanded to see the testimony of the trial. Rabin rejected their demand and they turned unsuccessfully to the Supreme Court to release the hidden testimony. This was the start of a campaign of repression against the families which included phone taps and threats. As one parent noted, "The IDF and government are treating us like the enemy because we want to know how our sons really died."

To appease an increasingly angry public, the Defense Ministry leaked an absurd scenario to a few selected reporters: the exercise at Tzeelim was a dry run for the assassination of Iraqi president Saddam Hussein. According to this scenario, Barak was going to lead a battalion of infantry, artillery, and rockets in an attack on Baghdad to get Hussein. Incredibly, a few compliant papers printed the nonsense.

Despite Barak's horrible reputation, Rabin began grooming him earlier this year for a political career that would end in his being Rabin's successor. The process began with a one-on-one high-level meeting with Warren Christopher in Jerusalem and culminated in a four-month trip from March to June to America during which he first conducted secret negotiations with the Syrians, then met Edgar Bronfman supposedly to finance a civilian career in high finance, and finally spent a few hours with Henry Kissinger for reasons never disclosed.

Those few journalists who had made the tie between Rabin's association with the Council on Foreign Relations and its leaders Edgar Bronfman and Henry Kissinger, understood then that Barak was being prepared to run Israel's diplomacy according to their agenda.

The grooming of Barak hit a major crisis in June when *Yediot Achronot* exposed his role in the Tzeelim Bet tragedy. But to give his side of matters, Barak went on a one-hour television special in which he ranted uncontrollably against his enemies in the army and the media. A short time later he was inducted by Rabin into his cabinet as interior minister. He held that post for only a month and a half before Rabin's assassination. President Clinton, former President Bush, and Secretary of State Warren Christopher reportedly implored the new Prime Minister Shimon Peres to advance Barak and Ramon and thus maintain the influence of the Council on Foreign Relations on Israeli diplomacy. Peres was given little chance but to obey, though he personally had little love or respect for either Barak or Ramon.

Ramon is best known for destroying the national labor union, the Histadrut, within a year of being appointed its secretary. To run for the position, he had to quit the Labor Party and his post of health minister, a decision that made little logical sense. Not many politicians walk out of a cabinet post to run a union, but he was amply funded from unknown sources and ran an American-style campaign which was ultimately successful.

For taking actions that utterly ruined the unions, Ramon was supposedly ostracized from Labor for good. But Rabin wanted him back, against the party consensus, and was preparing to reinvite him into his cabinet at the time of his assassination. When Peres was forced to accept him into his cabinet, Ramon was not even a member of the Labor Party.

However, he held some valuable secrets. According to the now defunct magazine *Haolam Hazeh*, in 1983 Ramon was given the task of recruiting a 23-year-old member of the Shas Party, Arye Deri, to the Labor fold. The strategy was devised by Peres who had lost two elections because the country's 600,000 Moroccans, the largest voting bloc, rejected him at the polls. If Shas with its six seats could be totally corrupted, the Moroccan vote could be had by Labor anyway. Two years later, Peres invited the 26-year-old unknown to be his minister of the interior. There he pillaged the budget. In 1990, then-Finance Minister Peres threatened to expose his crimes unless he joined Labor in felling the Shamir coalition. He used the same threats to get Shas to support the Oslo Accords three years later.

Deri was flattered by Ramon's attentions and started sharing contacts with him. The best known of the associates was Moshe Reich, a 38-year-old American-born electronics importer. He was charged in 1990 with cheating the state of $7.9 million in customs duty. At the time, he paid Ramon $50,000 to negotiate the sale of a mortgage bank. A few months later the charges against Reich were dropped, much to the shock of the judge and prosecutor who smelled a political favor. Reich was later investigated for giving Deri a $100,000 bribe for unknown reasons, but the police mysteriously closed their file on him in the midst of Deri's trial for corruption, fraud, and embezzlement.

Ramon's money ties to Deri carried on until the moment he was appointed the new interior minister. Ramon, as Histadrut secretary, sold off most of the union's properties for hundreds of millions of dollars. At the request of Deri, he appointed Moshe Habba, a Shas Party bigwig, as chairman of the company responsible for negotiating the sale of Histadrut assets.

The appointment of Barak as foreign minister and Ramon as interior minister will ensure that whatever Peres' future plans may be, Rabin's diplomatic reliance on the Council on Foreign Relations will continue as before.

Peres' First Acts

Shimon Peres wasted no time getting his agenda into full gear. He desecrated the shiva or seven-day mourning period of Yitzhak Rabin by selling parts of his country to Syria and the Vatican. Just hours after Yitzhak Rabin was safely buried, the race for the Golan Heights began. Arriving for the funeral were Prince Charles Windsor of the Royal Institute of International Affairs, who never publicly met Rabin, and his prime minister, John Major. They insisted Peres come to Orient House to make peace with Syria.

Peres turned the Brits down, but was far more compliant with the Americans. He promised Clinton that Syria could take over control of the South Lebanon security zone as part of the peace package. In effect, Peres sold the lives of the soldiers of the South Lebanese Army (SLA), who would fare no better under the Syrians than Arab collaborators with Israel have fared under the Palestinian Authority.

The promise not only ends the possibility of any Arab ever cooperating with Israel in the future, but opens a possible Syrian war front on the northern border, thus returning Israel completely to its 1948 lines.

Clinton was quite thrilled with the offer and two days later sent Dennis Ross shuttling between Peres and Assad. While Ross was in Damascus, twenty-five Katyushas fell on northern Israel from Lebanon. Whatever this message may have been, Peres refused to allow the IDF to respond with force as has been the pattern since his predecessor's failed Accountability Operation three years previously.

There is a most unexpected opponent to Peres' Golan diplo-

Prince Charles and British prime minister John Major at the funeral of Yitzhak Rabin.

macy. According to journalist Avinoam Bar-Yosef, the minister for the prime minister's affairs, Yossi Beilin, attempted to arrange a private meeting with Ross in Washington, but was turned down unless he coordinated it with Peres, which he refused to do. In response to the insult, Beilin leaked unpleasant information about Ross to the Israeli press. The Americans believe Beilin is trying to open his own Golan track behind Peres' back and he has the knowledge to be dangerous to many people including Ross, Warren Christopher, and U.S. ambassador to Israel, Martin Indyk.

And while the Golan was put up for immediate sale, Peres did not neglect his Vatican commitments. In September 1993 Peres signed a secret deal with the pope promising the Vatican hegemony over Jerusalem's Old City by the year 2000. Barely a month into power, the wheels of the Vatican deal started rolling.

The strategy chosen was to get Israelis used to their new friends in Rome. To further the "getting acquainted" period, Internal Security Minister Moshe Shachal refused to allow a Palestinian Authority meeting at the Vatican's Notre Dame Hospice in Jerusalem. According to Shachal, the Palestinians were planning to "use the Vatican to circumvent the Oslo Accords."

This odd incident was followed by the invitation offered to Leah Rabin and family to a private meeting with the pope. Ms. Rabin claimed that the pope had assured her that he considered Jerusalem the capital of Israel. The Vatican amended her announcement the next day with a complicated two-part formula which had Jerusalem both the capital of Israel and of Christendom.

Next came a trip to Jerusalem by the Vatican's secretary of state for foreign affairs, Archbishop Jean-Louis Tauran. While in the capital, the pope's representative addressed the Israeli branch of the Council on Foreign Relations headed by David Kimche, longtime Foreign Ministry office chief and a main architect of Iran-Contra. The pope, meanwhile, promised Tourism Minister Uri Baram that he will visit Jerusalem in the year 2000 and Mayor Ehud Olmert expressed his naive wishes that the trip would be sooner than that.

Peres got his chance to rule in November and by the new year, Israel's diplomacy had his mark deeply imbedded into it.

The Oslo Architects Target Jerusalem

Yair Hirschfeld and Ron Pundak, the two obscure academics who negotiated the first Oslo Accord, are at it again, and this time their main target is Jerusalem.

They are meeting secretly with Faisal el Husseini to cantonize the Holy City. El Husseini has already made a major "concession." He will permit Jews to go on living in the Jewish Quarter of the Old City.

According to the newspaper *Hatsofeh*, the scope of the talks is very broad. The trio are discussing giving Arab-populated regions of the Sharon and Galilee to the Palestinians, including the whole area known as the Triangle.

Hirschfeld's influential position is hardly accidental. In the 1970s he was a chief aide to Austrian president Bruno Kreisky, who was head of the Socialist International at the time. Kreisky was the Jew who obsessively attacked Prime Minister Menachem Begin calling him such epithets as "village shopkeeper."

While Kreisky was sworn to initiate the fall of Begin, he coordinated his activities with another member of the Socialist International, then-Israeli Labor Party chief Shimon Peres. Hirschfeld was sent to Israel to promote the agenda of the European branch of the movement to create a one-world government and quickly found a teaching position at Tel Aviv University. His leftist politics made him a friend of Palestinian and Israeli leftist leaders, especially Yossi Beilin and Palestinian leader Hanan Ashrawi. In November 1992 he was sent to a London hotel to meet PLO economics "minister" Abu Alah, and when the meeting ended, who just happened to be in the lobby "accidentally" but Beilin.

Hirschfeld just as "accidentally" reported on his meeting with

Abu Alah. Beilin liked what he heard, told Rabin, and thus was born the current peace process.

March 1996

> *Yehoshua Meiri, the Israeli journalist who informed the editors about the illegal deal by the Labor Party and the PLO to rig the 1992 elections, described a scenario in early February 1996 which concluded that "all hell would break loose" if Peres didn't revert to his previous NWO allegiances. Within a week, a bombing wave erupted which eventually killed fifty-nine people and wounded over two hundred. It also signalled the end of Peres' career, one would hope.*

New World Order Rivalry Spelled Rabin's Doom

Israeli radio journalist Yehoshua Meiri postulates that Yitzhak Rabin's murder was the result of a New World Order rivalry. Rabin had accepted Henry Kissinger's plan for a new Middle East to be created by bribery. America was set to release $42 billion of Iranian funds frozen in American banks since 1979 on condition that Iran cease all hostile activities against Israel. Another $38 billion was to be distributed among radical states and organizations such as Sudan, Syria, Libya, Hamas, Islamic Jihad, etc. in return for a final peace with Israel and an alliance with the U.S. The grand Middle East peace treaty would be signed at the White House by all the states of the region.

The European sponsors of Shimon Peres panicked as the plan inched toward fruition. Such a Middle East/American alliance would have left Europe out in the cold and threatened its energy supply and economy. Europe's plan for Israel was very different. It was to be at the forefront of a worldwide battle against Islamic extremists led by Jordan and Egypt.

"Rabin's assassination short-circuited the Kissinger plan," adds

Meiri, "and the most powerful advocates like Bush, Carter, and Clinton rushed to his funeral and forced Peres to accept Ehud Barak as his foreign minister. If Peres doesn't play ball, watch out for Barak as the Labor candidate for the elections. And if the radicals don't get their promised payoff very soon, all hell will break out in Israel."

Peres, meanwhile, has commitments in Europe to people like Chancellor Kohl, Roland Dumas, and the pope. In a recent visit to Germany, Peres disappeared for two hours and later claimed he visited a dentist. Meiri insists he met the Iranians who pressed him on the Rabin deal. That evening the German foreign minister flew to Iran, under cover of saving downed pilot Ron Arad, and tried to strike a balance to keep Peres in power and alive.

Peres, meanwhile, is paying heavy lip service to the Kissinger plan and announced that when a peace treaty was reached, twenty Moslem countries would sign it on the White House lawn.

Kissinger protegé and fellow Council on Foreign Relations executive Edgar Bronfman is a primary activist for keeping the Rabin diplomacy alive. In a January interview with *Maariv* reporter Yitzhak Ben Horin, Bronfman admitted to using his influence to secure Rabin's election in 1992 because

> he was a brilliant strategist. I helped him become prime minister. Usually I believe Americans should not interfere with the Israeli election infrastructure, but in this case I broke my rule because I believed in the peace process.

The question is how he could have believed in Rabin's peace process before the elections when it didn't exist. While running for prime minister, Rabin insisted he would never withdraw from the Golan Heights or negotiate with the PLO.

In January, the same Bronfman who used his influence to make Rabin prime minister because of a peace process that Rabin supposedly developed after he was elected, personally persuaded President Clinton to add sanctions on Iran until it ceased its terror campaign against Israel.

Concludes Meiri: "Peres can't abandon Europe, but it's too dangerous to give up on the Kissinger plan. That's why he called elections. It was a way out. He knows or strongly suspects who was behind Rabin's murder. He has debts to pay if he wants to survive."

The Labor government's policy of providing a refuge for thieves from behind the former Iron Curtain reaches an apex as Peres and Shachal bag a president.

Peres Sinks Deeper Into the Liaison Department Mire

For several months in 1992, Rabin's killer, Yigal Amir, worked for a covert division of the prime minister's office called the Liaison Department. The purpose of this department is to recruit Jews from the CIS to immigrate to Israel. Amir was sent to Riga, Latvia, supposedly as a Hebrew teacher. There has been endless speculation about Amir's real purpose in Latvia or what was done to him there.

Shortly after Rabin's murder, Peres announced that because of financial irregularities, he would close down the Liaison Office. But after a meeting with Yossi Kedmi, head of the department, Peres changed his mind and agreed to continued financing of the strange operation. However, he appointed his legal affairs advisor, Achaz Ben Ari, to oversee Kedmi.

Then two events exposed the seriousness of the department's activities. In late December an Israeli spy was arrested in Moscow. The Russians claimed he worked "for a division of the Prime Minister's Office," which must have been the Liaison Office. The spy was deported to Israel, where he was promoted.

The next incident is more complicated and insidious. The *Haaretz* headline of January 23, 1996, read: "Suspicion That CIS

Criminals Received Immigration Visas from the Liaison Office."
The article explained that the police were investigating suspicions
that members of the Russian mafia entered Israel via the Liaison
Department offices behind the former Iron Curtain.

Enter the most famous such criminal of all, former Ukrainian
president Yafim Zviagilski. In June 1994, just prior to the Ukrainian elections, Peres and Moshe Shachal flew to the Ukraine for a
long meeting with Zviagilski. In October, three months later,
Zviagilski, now defeated in the elections, arrived in Israel on phony
immigration papers claiming citizenship based on his being Jewish, which he is not. He brought with him $30 million pilfered
from the Ukrainian treasury.

In January, the Ukrainian government sued the Israeli government in an Israeli court to have Zviagilski extradited, and Peres
said he would personally work on speeding up the resolution of
the issue. And who was Zviagilski's attorney? Tzvi Hefetz, the legal affairs adviser of the Liaison Office.

Shachal is not happy about something and has doubled his
own personal security and introduced plans to add 13,000 new
men to the Israel police force because of a seemingly irrational
fear of the Russian mafia. There is much more to the Liaison Office than meets the eye and one journalist is pursuing the longshot
possibility that Rabin's murder was a Russian mafia hit.

May 1996

*New World Order intrigue leads Peres into a small war and out of
the Prime Minister's Office.*

Why Operation Grapes of Wrath?

One night in mid-April a Lebanese boy was allegedly hurt by a
bomb. The bomb was not Israeli, but this was the flimsy pretext
that supposedly led to a Hizbollah attack and many others dur-

ing a failed IDF mini-war called Grapes of Wrath.

After seventeen days of wrathful grapes, Israel agreed to a cease-fire that changed nothing, even after 1,250 homes in Galilee were damaged.

The question no one in the Israeli or foreign media asked is: Why did Hizbollah choose to abrogate its 1993 agreement with Israel not to fire rockets into northern Israel in the first place? The answer, of course, is New World Order (NWO) covert diplomacy. The Syrian-Iranian axis is allied to the French-German branch of the NWO whose major components are the Socialist International, old money, and the Vatican. It is this branch which has been building Iran's sophisticated weapons program.

Until the assassination of Yitzhak Rabin, this was the NWO branch which controlled Shimon Peres. But after Rabin's murder, George Bush, Jimmy Carter, Prince Charles, and Bill Clinton made it very clear to Peres that they would not tolerate any change to Rabin's Anglo-Saxon NWO alliance. To strengthen their hold on the Israeli government, Peres was forced to take Rabin's protegés, Ehud Barak and Haim Ramon, into his cabinet.

In February, Peres received his first strong messages. After London talks between Israelis and Hamas sponsored by the Royal Institute for International Affairs reached a deadlock, five suicide bombers killed fifty-nine people in Jerusalem, Tel Aviv, and Ashkelon.

In the wake of the carnage Barak, Ramon, and Yossi Beilin (who planned Oslo with Rabin) met to discuss a *putsch*. Peres was to be replaced by Barak as defense minister and Beilin was supposed to take over as foreign minister. With Ramon already interior minister, the Anglo-Saxon triumvirate would have had effective control over Israel.

Peres understood the threat and agreed to switch his allegiances away from Europe. This the Europeans would not abide and they ordered Hizbollah into action. According to Ben Caspit writing in *Maariv,* the Belgian ambassador to Lebanon reported a meeting (just before the Katyushas fell on Israel) between the secretary of Hizbollah, Sheikh Khasan Nasrallah, and a delegation from President Assad to "coordinate joint operations."

Forced into a war he didn't want, Peres ordered the IDF to fire shells and missiles, but not to actually challenge the enemy on the ground. The strategy inevitably led to Lebanese civilian losses, and while they piled up, the French foreign ministry was in Damascus brokering an agreement with President Assad, while the Italian foreign minister toured Lebanon to reinforce the European NWO pressure.

In the end, the elite from the Anglo-American alliance prevailed over Peres. Peres realized the danger posed to him if he didn't relent, but we have not heard the last of the Europeans.

Confirmation is received of Inside Israel's *contention that the bombing wave of February/March was directly due to Peres' secret diplomacy.*

The Secret Meetings

According to the secretary of the Palestinian Authority, Taib Abd el-Rahim, quoted in the Egyptian newspaper *Al-Hayat*, "Shimon Peres informed the leadership of the PA that in January he opened secret talks with Hamas."

Al-Hayat added that the Hamas leadership in Gaza knew nothing of the talks and they were apparently taking place with Hamas bigshots in London. In March, *Maariv*'s London correspondent reported that the wave of suicide bombs within Israel had nothing to do with the death of "The Engineer" as was generally thought, but resulted from a breakdown in the secret London talks.

Meanwhile, the weekly *Kol Hair* claimed the opposite. While agreeing that secret talks led to the bombing wave, it reprinted an agreement between Israeli negotiators led by Rabbi David Froman of Tekoah and Hamas leaders Dr. Mahmud A-Zaar and Sheikh Hamil Khamami. Hamas agreed to stop all terrorism in return for the release of their founder, Sheikh Ahmad Yassin, from prison.

Shimon Peres agreed to do so and the London Hamas branch retaliated with suicide bombers.

The PLO opened its own channel to the Jewish residents of Judea, Samaria, and Gaza. A group of five settler leaders, including most surprisingly Rabbi Eliezer Waldman, organized by former head of the Institute of Strategic Studies at Tel Aviv University, Joseph Alper, have had a series of meetings with PLO leaders, including one "outside Oxford at the home of a Jew who arranges and pays for these kinds of talks." Most likely, Lord Victor Mishkon.

The PLO-Hamas Treaty

MK Benny Begin presented Shimon Peres with documented proof that last January in Cairo, Yasser Arafat cut a deal with the Hamas that gave the latter terror group free reign to kill as many Israelis as it wants, just so long as it operates from outside the boundaries of the Palestinian Authority.

Peres, naturally, lied and denied that any such agreement had taken place. But once again he was caught up in his deceit when the PLO's past-ambassador to the Arab League, Mahmud Tzvayakh, told an Egyptian television reporter that the recent terror wave came out of the Hebron region in keeping with the agreement between Arafat and Hamas signed earlier in Cairo.

In the wake of the agreement Arafat appointed a Hamas sheikh, Muhmad Abu Zair, as mufti of Jenin. Further, he now includes a reference in all his public speeches to "my brother, the leader of Hamas, Sheikh Ahmad Yassin."

To make matters more complicated, *Maariv*'s Washington reporter Avinoam Bar Yosef reported that American intelligence sources have proof that the money to finance the bombing wave came from Jordan, and that Jordan has funneled over $170 million to Hamas over the past year.

Despite these facts, well known to the government, Tourism

Minister Uzi Baram has begun a campaign to repay Jordan for "their properties in Jerusalem."

Clearly Peres' demise was in the air and that may explain the rush to fulfill the New World Order agenda.

No one should be surprised by Bibi's shaking of Arafat's hand in September 1996. In the May 1996 issue, Inside Israel *reported that Netanyahu announced that he was prepared to meet with Yasser Arafat. The announcement was made at a meeting of the Israeli Council on Foreign Relations, the foreign policy think-tank that the Rockefeller's finance and control.*

July 1996

For the past year, Inside Israel *had been collecting disturbing information on Binyamin Netanyahu's secret ties. They, it appeared, were little different than Rabin's.*

The editors welcomed his election despite the evidence that the Council on Foreign Relations controlled the new prime minister. His coalition would be far less compliant than the previous government. Still, as the youth anthem goes, "We won't be fooled again."

Who Is Binyamin Netanyahu?

Two Fridays after Israel's new prime minister was elected, the newspapers were filled with bios of the new leader. The most in-depth research was undertaken by Orly Azula-Katz, Anat Meidan, and Rami Tal of *Yediot Achronot* who produced a balanced portrait, and Biranit Goren of *Kol Hair* whose story was a snow job.

Nonetheless, both reports agreed in most details, if not interpretations. These two reports, combined with other public knowledge, create a most disturbing and mysterious caricature of Israel's leader for students of secret diplomacy.

The Conventional Story

The prevailing myth about Prime Minister Binyamin Netanyahu is that he grew up in a highly politicized, right-wing household. Responsibility for the presumption lies with his father, Bar Tzion, a dedicated revisionist who was a pallbearer at the funeral of Zeev Jabotinsky.

The facts are different. Netanyahu recalls," My father did not want me to enter politics. We were very nonpolitical." The founding families of Zionism's revisionist wing which produced two generations of leaders like Menachem and Benny Begin and Yaacov and Dan Meridor, barely knew of the Netanyahus.

What Binyamin inherited from his father was an obsession with learning. His grades in junior high were all above average but he excelled in only one subject: music.

When Binyamin moved to America at age fourteen after his father accepted a teaching post in Philadelphia, his hero became JFK. Netanyahu felt very alienated being away from Israel and took waitering jobs to earn the money to spend his summers back home. There his greatest pleasure was working on left-wing kibbutzim with his pals from Jerusalem. They recall that he would always try to outwork them, even when he had an injured knee.

Returning to high school in Philadelphia, Netanyahu shared close friendship with only those students as imbued with love for Israel as he was. He was a straight-A student who graduated fourth in his class at Cheltenham High School, one of the most academically competitive schools in America. But he didn't attend his graduation ceremony. War broke out on June 5, 1967, and Netanyahu flew to Israel to volunteer for the army.

A high school buddy, Ari Bintener recalls, "No one was surprised. It was obvious his place was in Israel. I was pleased that he found a way to help his country."

Bob Trimble, Netanyahu's soccer coach, remembers, "Bibi was the best player on the team, except for his brother Yoni who could have played professionally if he had wanted to. The only problem with Ben was that his political views were so far to the left of the other players."

As a soldier, Binyamin rose to the rank of captain in the most secret combat unit of all, the fighting arm of military intelligence. He took part in a good number of legendary operations and was wounded while fighting hijackers holding a Sabena passenger plane. On the Suez, he almost drowned trying to swim with his heavy automatic rifle under Egyptian fire. He became known as "the lousy swimmer from Jerusalem."

Soldiers recall him as a cool but "square" officer who lost his temper only once. That was when he found his men had been taking "souvenirs" from operations in Lebanon. He put a quick end to what he viewed as looting.

After five years of soldiering Netanyahu returned to America to study architecture at either Harvard or MIT. He chose the latter because it permitted him to begin an MA course load, as his academic advisor Prof. Leon Garviser remembers. "I told him that no one could handle the load, but he insisted that he had to make up for time lost while serving his country. I agreed to add one extra course in the first semester and when he passed all his courses I added another one. In the end he finished his MA in two and a half years. Don't ask me how. No one did it before him or since."

Once again, Netanyahu interrupted his studies only once. In October of 1973 war broke out in Israel and he flew back to fight in the Sinai. When he returned, he became a student activist on behalf of Israel, a fact that was noted by the Israeli consul of Boston, Collette Avital. In one of the many ironies in his life, it was Avital, the dovish consul of New York during the Rabin/Peres administration who arranged Netanyahu's first television appearance, a debate with PLO activist Prof. Edward Said.

The loss of his brother Yoni during the Entebbe raid put a stop to Binyamin's plans to become an architect. Instead he settled for an MA in business administration and took a post at the Boston Consulting Group. His boss was Ira Magaziner, the man who later was the intellectual force behind the Clinton administration's failed health reform package.

As Moshe Arens notes, "Bibi is only the second prime minister who ever had a real job outside the army or politics. Shamir was the first. He once worked as an accountant in a glue factory."

While working at Boston Consulting, Binyamin received his first diplomatic assignment: he was sent to Sweden to advise the government on efficient administration of public companies.

Already earning $100,000 and with a splendid career before him, Netanyahu decided to give it all up and return to Israel to act as the marketing manager of a furniture concern. As his colleague Barbara Maclogan notes, "Anyone who claims Bibi planned to live in America doesn't know what he's talking about. He gave up the opportunity of his life in Boston to earn a quarter of his salary in Israel."

In 1979, Netanyahu organized an antiterrorism conference in Jerusalem, dedicated to his fallen brother. He managed to attract the likes of George Bush, George Shultz, and Richard Perle (President Reagan's chief arms negotiator) to the meeting and was thrust briefly onto the world stage. But when the conference ended, it was back to work at the furniture factory.

That all changed in 1982 when Israel's Washington ambassador, Moshe Arens, invited Netanyahu to be his deputy. This unprecedented career rise has been a subject of much speculation. Many people have noted that Bar Tzion Netanyahu was one of the few guests invited to Arens' wedding and he was repaying an old friend. But Arens has a different explanation. "People got a good laugh when they heard I phoned a furniture factory to find a deputy. What sold me on Bibi was his organization of the anti-terror conference and the strong impression he made on American leaders who participated."

In 1984, after two visibly successful years as Arens' deputy, Bibi was named Israel's ambassador to the U.N. In another of those ironies that follow him, he was appointed to the post by Shimon Peres against the objections of Yitzhak Shamir. Once again, it was a leader of the Labor Party who promoted his early career.

This was the true turning point in his quest to become prime minister. Netanyahu's good looks, fluent English, and controversial opinions made him a media star. He became a frequent presence on Ted Koppel's "Nightline" and "Larry King Live." As King observes, "Whenever he appeared, the phones wouldn't stop ringing. He especially made an impression on women viewers. As a guest I'd rate him eight. If he had a sense of humor to go with everything else, he'd have been a ten."

During this period, Netanyahu wrote his book, *Terror: How The West Can Win*. The book made a tremendous impression on the Reagan administration. In fact, whenever George Shultz visited New York, and that was often, he would call on Netanyahu.

By 1988, Netanyahu had made powerful allies in the American media. He received strong support from Charles Krauthammer of the *Washington Post*, Abe Rosenthal of the *New York Times*, and Ellie Weymouth, daughter of Katherine Graham, the publisher of *Newsweek*. When he returned to Israel, he was too powerful a figure to be ignored and was appointed first deputy foreign minister and later the prime minister's spokesman. In this capacity, CNN made Netanyahu an international media star during the Persian Gulf War.

Netanyahu was ready to challenge the Old Guard of the Likud. The combination of youth, determination, and powerful allies abroad led to a resounding victory in the Likud primaries of 1993 and in the general elections of 1996.

The Secret Life of Binyamin Netanyahu

Even within the conventional story, it is clear that Netanyahu was groomed for leadership by the Council on Foreign Relations (CFR) in New York. In 1979, 27-year-old Netanyahu called a conference on terrorism and the ruling elite of the CFR—Bush, Shultz and

Perle—answered his summons. One word will suffice: why? Yoni Netanyahu was undoubtedly a martyr, but far from the only one in Israel. He was not such a powerful symbol that the CFR would send a delegation of its biggest guns, including CIA director Bush, to his unknown brother's get-together.

Netanyahu's decision to quit his lucrative Boston job is almost inexplicable. Netanyahu sought a high paying job at a prestigious consulting firm, yet not two months later he gave it up to fly back to Israel and sell sofas. He was barely settled in back home when he decided to organize an antiterrorism conference and invite the most powerful people in Washington to attend.

It is possible that Netanyahu was told to quit his job, return to Israel, and arrange the conference. Perhaps there is a connection to the fact that a year later Shultz later made fighting terrorism a first priority of the Reagan administration and that Vice-President Bush was appointed to head a front for illegal covert activities called the Anti-Terror Task Force.

Arens' offer of a deputy ambassadorship to salesman Netanyahu made no political sense. Israeli diplomatic aides and deputies typically rise slowly through the Foreign Ministry bureaucracy. They are not thrust into the second highest position at the most vital embassy in the world. It is far from impossible that Arens was directed to bring in Netanyahu by the very people in the Reagan administration who attended his conference three years earlier.

Once in New York in 1984, CFR-affiliated media such as CNN, the *New York Times, Washington Post, Newsweek,* and CFR members Koppel and King turned Netanyahu into a major political figure; so much so that George Shultz became a close friend. We again ask the succinct question: why? What did Shultz, twenty years Netanyahu's senior, find so amusing about the Israeli U.N. ambassador that he had to pay him a courtesy call every time he flew to New York? In 1985, Shultz chaired another Netanyahu-organized conference on terrorism, this time in Washington. The resulting publicity and prestige was a significant factor in

Netanyahu's fast-rising political career. Clearly, the secretary of state had a major stake in Netanyahu's future. Which means, so did George Bush.

All that can be concluded from the conventional story. What then do we make of Bibi's secret life?

In 1987, Netanyahu applied for credit using his American social security number 020-36-4537. With that number, he or someone else made the application under a phony name, John Sullivan, living at a false address in northern California.

Netanyahu used Sullivan's name to borrow money during 1987 and 1988. John Sullivan does not exist, nor does Netanyahu's credit file. Israeli and American reporters who tried to dig into Netanyahu's past using his social security number discovered two other phony names used to apply for credit in 1987 and 1988, but were perplexed to find that his credit records were completely removed. Only someone very high up in the American government could have authorized the erasing of the file.

We return to the all-purpose question: why? Again, no one who knows is talking. What is nearly certain is that while Netanyahu was the U.N. ambassador, he was either defrauding a credit company or on an assignment involving money that required three identity changes.

Then there is Netanyahu's close relationship with Congressman Ben Gillman, head of the House Committee on International Relations. The problem here is that Gillman was also a close associate of Shabtai Kalmonovitch and shared business deals with him in Africa. Kalmonovitch was later imprisoned in Israel as a KGB spy. This is not to imply that Netanyahu was involved in spying, only that his closest ally in Congress has mighty strange intelligence ties to Israel.

And what to make of the mystery of Netanyahu's housing. Before he was even the leader of the Likud, two foreign businessmen, Jack Mandel of Australia and Sandy Eisenstadt of the U.S., each paid about $750,000 to buy Netanyahu luxury apartments in Tel Aviv and Jerusalem. Again, no one has a clue why. There is speculation that part of the reason may be Eisenstadt's stake in an Israeli oil exploration company, a shady and hidden business, but no concrete connection has been discovered by the Israeli media.

Netanyahu's penchant for secrecy is not subtle. It is well-known among the Israeli media that he had conducted a number of secret meetings with the Jordanian royal family in London and Amman before he became prime minister. Even the conventional *Jerusalem Post* reported in mid-June that six secret meetings were held in the past two years. But when *Inside Israel* just before the elections asked Netanyahu to comment on the meetings, he denied they had ever taken place.

Perhaps the most secret and worrying ties concern what is supposedly a high-tech services company. *Yediot Achronot* relates how Netanyahu wooed a local Likud leader. "He was invited by Netanyahu to a meeting in his office at Systematics in Ramat Gan. The head of the company, Oded Levental, is a candidate for a financial post in the new government."

Systematics is at the core of serious research by American alternative publications, including the usually reliable Media Bypass. In short, the allegations are that the National Security Agency had handed Systematics stolen software called PROMIS that opened a trap door to the world's secret banking transactions. About 250 Americans, mostly politicians, had their illegal foreign accounts emptied of over $3.5 billion in the operation. It is claimed that Colin Powell dropped out of the presidential race after his account electronically vanished. Leading figures in the operation included George Bush, Caspar Weinberger, and two Arkansas attorneys, Vince Foster Jr. and Hillary Rodham Clinton on behalf of Clinton financier Jackson Stephens. The research invariably concludes that Foster was murdered because he knew too much about the scam.

A leading investigative writer, Sherman Skolnick, writes:

Some contend Systematics is an NSA proprietary and spies on

banks overseas. Can Systematics rightfully deny spying actually done by buffers or cutouts between Systematics and NSA? Systematics, through a spokesperson, vigorously denies Foster assisted it in any spying on foreign banks but remains apparently silent on whether Hillary Rodham Clinton assisted Systematics in some nefarious activities.

Is it fair to ask why Systematics provided Netanyahu office space and if this was the sum total of its involvement with him?

Since taking office, Netanyahu has fueled fears of international control by his actions within Israel's tiny anti-NWO community. They were most intrigued by his refusal to give Ariel Sharon a sensitive cabinet post. One possible reason is fear of Sharon's own intelligence arm in the U.S. Then for those people who fervently hoped that he would rid himself of any connections to the Arye Deri scandal, with all its implications of money laundering and perhaps murder, Netanyahu appointed as his justice minister Yaacov Neeman, a lawyer who is currently being investigated for intimidating a key witness against Deri in a London trial.

But the topper was Netanyahu's decision to allow Yaacov Frenkel to run the country's economy single-handedly. Frenkel worked for the World Bank between 1971 and 1990. After nineteen years away from "home" Frenkel was unex-plainably appointed head of the Bank of Israel.

His policies mirrored the worldwide debt program of his previous employer documented by numerous researchers. The plan involves raising interest rates beyond what the public or industry can afford, and forcing the government to borrow lots of money from American banks to keep the populace pacified. When the debts have to be repaid from an empty treasury, the International Monetary Fund bails out the country with schemes guaranteed to impoverish the people.

Frenkel was a proponent of Israel borrowing $10 billion in loans guaranteed by the American government and he kept his interest rates as high as he could in the face of opposition from then-Finance Minister Avraham Shohat who suspected Frenkel "was playing politics with the Bank of Israel."

Binyamin Netanyahu, the man who *Inside Israel* hoped would save Israel from the NWO puppet regime of Peres, appointed Yaacov Frenkel to be his minister of finance. The only thing that prevented the disaster was party opposition to an appointee who had never publicly supported the Likud.

Dan Meridor got the post instead. But as the *Maariv* headline read: "Meridor Will Act, Frenkel Will Lead." On his first day in office Meridor announced that his policy would be to lower the standard of living in Israel. Not a week later, Frenkel raised the interest rates by a whopping 1.5 percent with Meridor's "approval."

Something is going on behind the scenes at the CFR. While Secretary of State Warren Christopher must appear to be opposing Likud government policies to keep the Arabs in line, the former CFR director is playing some kind of double game with Netanyahu.

King Hussein made his accommodation with Netanyahu well before the elections and refused to support Peres during the campaign. Netanyahu's victory clearly delighted him and on the surface, why not? The last thing he would want is a PLO state on his border with control of the Moslem holy sites. In time, it will become clearer what Netanyahu promised the king during the secret London meetings. Included, most assuredly, will be Jordanian hegemony over the Temple Mount.

There has been a transformation in Israel, but the CFR is still running the latest prime minister, and that is a good reason for intense fear about Israel's future.

If proof was needed that the Illuminati is active in Israel, the following report provides it. It is based on an article which appeared in Davar Rishon *on May 8, 1996, and a report on Israel TV on May 7.*

Masons Busted in Tel Aviv

On May 6, Tel Aviv police were joined in a raid on an apartment by reporters from the state-run television evening news program and a reporter from the daily newspaper *Davar Rishon*. Once the police knocked down the door, the cameras captured a most bizarre scene. The walls were covered in Latin script, skulls and bones graced the shelves, and crossed swords were mounted above and beside an altar. Five doors led to secret passageways, with blinking red lights signalling to whoever was within that intruders were present.

The next day, both the television news and *Davar Rishon* reported that neighbors had complained to the police that a cult had occupied an apartment in their building. To the shock of the police, according to the news report, "the apartment was used for ceremonies by the Freemasons, an organization whose membership boasts cabinet ministers and high ranking army officers."

In fact, neighbors had not complained to the police. The snitch was Yehoshua Meiri, one of the best-known investigative journalists in the Hebrew press. Meiri was the senior Arab affairs reporter for two of the most prestigious daily newspapers, *Maariv* and *Haaretz*. He spent five years in Cairo as a correspondent, built many contacts in even the most radical Islamic groups, and became privy to the behind-the-scenes machinations of Middle East diplomacy.

However he managed it, in March 1994 Meiri published a bombshell in the newspaper *Hadashot*. He claimed, with no small amount of backup tapes, that Shimon Peres had rigged the 1992 general elections in a plot concocted with Secretary of State James Baker. In short, he offered Arafat a deal: if he used his influence to recruit Israeli/Arab voters to the Labor coalition, he would be rewarded with a state when Labor rose to power. This was the genesis of the Middle East peace process which is clearly aimed at destroying Israel.

But Peres was replaced by Yitzhak Rabin as party leader and

thus, Israel was dubiously rewarded with an active Mason leading the country.

A few months after Meiri's exposé, two Israeli publications, *Yediot Achronot* and *Shishi*, published long articles extolling the contribution of Masonry to Israeli society. Both reports contained items about Rabin's association with the organization and they agreed in detail. Rabin had been a Mason since the late 1960s.

Rabin's office issued the same statement to both papers: "Just prior to becoming ambassador to Washington in 1968, General Rabin joined the Masons as a diplomatic courtesy. He has not been active since." Both papers noted that the statement was not entirely accurate: In 1976 Rabin presided over a large Masonic convention in Jerusalem and there are archive photos to prove it. Then there is another problem with the official explanation: What kind of a diplomatic courtesy to America is joining the Masons?

The weekly newspaper *Shishi* reported that Likud opposition leader Binyamin Netanyahu was also said to be a Mason. He was recruited when he was Israel's ambassador to the U.N. in the 1980s. Both newspapers observed that King Hussein of Jordan was a high-ranking and proud Mason who travelled to London often to participate in ceremonies.

Once in Washington, Rabin fell heavily into the grasp of National Security Advisor Henry Kissinger. This isn't the place to provide the evidence but almost certainly Kissinger forced Golda Meir to resign as prime minister during the contrived Yom Kippur War in favor of Rabin, and just as certainly, Kissinger, Rabin, and Syrian president Hafez el Assad ignited the Lebanon civil war in 1975 with the compliance of Jordan's King Hussein.

But if there was any doubt of Rabin's secret society ties, the Masons themselves chose to remove it. In November 1994 President Clinton flew to Israel to finalize a peace agreement with Jordan. After the treaty was signed, Clinton, Rabin, and Hussein posed for the cliched "all join hands" photo. This shot appeared in full page ads two days later in Israel's newspapers. The headline read: "MASONS OF PEACE." After Rabin was murdered, Ephraim Fuchs, the Grand Master of the Grand Lodge of Israeli Masonry, thoughtfully published ads mourning the passing of "a brother."

In February 1995, the editors of *Inside Israel* interviewed a Palestinian reporter for a London-based Saudi-financed Arabic newspaper, *Mahmud Abu Eid*. When the conspiratorial side of the peace process was brought up he replied, "Oh, you mean the Mason thing."

He continued: "Do you think Hussein would ever have signed the treaty if Israel didn't secretly give him future control of the Moslem holy sites in Jerusalem? Palestinians are opposed to the agreement because we know we lost out. And if Hussein did get control, then the Masons got their foothold on the Temple Mount."

The Masons covet the Temple Mount, site of Solomon's Temple, because their mythology has the organization being established by one Hiram, the mason who supposedly built the temple three thousand years ago.

The very day the Jordanian treaty was signed, Rabin flew off to London on an unspecified mission. Three weeks before the agreement was signed, Netanyahu had been in London. Shortly after the signing ceremony ended, he was in Amman. Netanyahu offered no opposition to the agreement's highly questionable water or territorial concessions or its secret clauses on Jerusalem. As even the Grand Master of Israel's Grand Lodge subtly suggested, the treaty between Jordan and Israel was organized by the Masons.

In October 1995, the Italian publication *Le Republica* reported on the hold Masonry has over Israel's leadership. Naturally, the Rabin evidence was presented, but another name also popped up: former Jerusalem mayor, Teddy Kollek.

In February 1995, David Rockefeller visited Jerusalem for half a day and flew out. His quickie visit, the first in over twenty years, was leaked to and reported throughout the Israeli press. He came to have a meeting with Teddy Kollek. The doddering Kollek explained afterwards that Rockefeller was exploring setting up a branch of the Chase Manhattan Bank in Jerusalem. The transparency of this lie is unworthy of comment but two events did follow, one perhaps coincidental, the other surely not. The day after the visit, PLO forces shot dead 28 protesters in Gaza. Within a week, Kollek took his first ever trip to Egypt and presented Foreign Minister Omar Moussa with a plan created by a semi-secret organization he founded, the Jerusalem Forum, for the upcoming division of the city into cantons. The Israeli press reported that the plan, called Metropolitan Jerusalem, was presented for Egyptian government approval.

We return now to the Tel Aviv apartment bust. After *Davar Rishon* printed the article, Ephraim Fuchs, grand master of the local Grand Lodge, issued a most enlightening statement. He claimed that the apartment was rented by a cult called the Illuminati, which had nothing to do with Freemasonry. He demanded a published apology.

Yehoshua Meiri gave the reporter from *Davar Rishon* my number and I gave her a potted history of Adam Weishaupt and the Illuminati. The next day I was quoted on the front page saying the Illuminati was part of Freemasonry.

An afterword: *Davar Rishon* was shut down for good within two weeks. It suffered publicized financial problems, so the two events are probably unrelated. The Masonic manipulation of the blood-soaked Middle East peace process is not.

After swallowing their shocking fall from power, the editors of Inside Israel *were relieved to see that the Israeli left finally became a tad conspiratorial.*

Did Peres Deliberately Lose the Election?

Television cameraman Alon Eilat says, "Peres was so torn between the threats of the American and European powerbrokers that he lost the election to escape."

While not sharing Eilat's motive, after the elections the Israeli media widely speculated that Peres did indeed throw the election. Reporters asked why Peres chose Ehud Barak and Haim Ramon to run his campaign. Both were solidly in Rabin's camp and Barak was already groomed by Rabin's American controllers to be his successor. With any number of his own supporters to choose from, the selection of Ramon and Barak was not logical.

Together, the journalists contend, Ramon and Barak sabotaged Peres' chances. Public relations experts agreed that the campaign slogan, "Israel Is Strong with Peres," was the worst possible message. It served as a daily reminder that Israel was in fact not looking very strong at all.

According to a close Peres aide quoted by Vered Levi-Barzilai in the weekly *Yerushalayim*, "Peres received accurate polls that he could lose, but would not listen to advice on how to win. He simply froze."

Another close aide agreed: "Ramon was clearly unsuitable for the job, but when Peres was advised to get someone else, he froze. He was terrified of Ramon's reaction. That was the start of his continuing paralysis. He lost control of the situation."

Concludes Levi-Barzilai, "Peres was enclosed in his own world. A hammer blow to the head couldn't have snapped him back to

Masonic handshake between Yitzhak Rabin and Yassir Arafat

reality. He was overwhelmed with fear."

Peres constantly maintained that outside forces, especially Iran, were deliberately sabotaging his chances for victory. In the wake of his defeat, Hizbollah leader Khassan Nasrallah justified Peres' contention saying, "Not only was Operation Grapes of Wrath a failure, but we got the Labor Party and its leader Peres out of the way." He concluded by condemning President Clinton for aiding Peres to bomb Lebanese civilians.

Chapter Nine

October 1996

Dr. Dore Gold: Slave of Kissinger

In early July, Henry Kissinger organized a conference in Amman aimed at determining the future of the Middle East after the year 2000. Invited were a fine collection of New World Order leaders including Simone Weil, past-president of the E.U. parliament, and Lord Rothschild of London. Kissinger extended invitations to the following Israelis:

- Yaacov Frenkel, who worked for the World Bank in Washington from 1971 to 1990 and is now doing its handiwork as head of the Bank of Israel.
- Ronnie Milo, the renegade Likud MK who refused to vote against the Declaration of Principles with the PLO in 1993 and is now negotiating over the future of Jerusalem with the PLO's Faisal el Husseini.
- Meir Shamgar, the former chief justice of the Supreme Court who led commissions which whitewashed the Rabin assassination and Hebron massacre of 1994.
- Yossi Beilin, the architect of Oslo.
- Dr. Dore Gold, Prime Minister Netanyahu's ghoulish political advisor.

After deciding the future of the region, Dr. K flew to Jerusalem in the private jet of Conrad Black, CEO of the Hollinger Corporation, owner of the *Jerusalem Post*. There he met privately with Netanyahu despite his request that aide Yvet Lieberman join them in their meeting. After two hours, Netanyahu left the meeting, his face blanched, and refused to say one word to reporters. As one witness noted, "This was a man who looked like he'd been intimidated."

Kissinger next visited the *Jerusalem Post* building where the publisher updated him on former editor David Bar Ilan's departure to become Netanyahu's media advisor. Dr. K told reporters there: "The new prime minister must be made to realize that the peace process is good for Israel."

Kissinger returned to America and published a policy piece in the *Los Angeles Times* outlining his views on how negotiations with the Syrians must be conducted. Not a month later *Yediot Achronot* reported on Dr. Dore Gold's new approach to negotiations with the Syrians and surprise, surprise, they duplicated Kissinger's own. According to the report:

> Very quietly, under a heavy cloak of secrecy, the Prime Minister's
> Office is planning to bring about the renewal of negotiations
> with the Syrians. . . . Dr. Dore Gold conceived the plan, based
> on Kissinger's Helsinki model for Europe during the 1970s.

Gold's plan calls for renewing discussions at the Wye Plantation, a facility owned by the Council on Foreign Relations' (CFR) sister organization, the Aspen Institute. The goal will be to set up a number of "baskets" or committees to defuse regional tensions. The committees will be chaired alternatively between the U.S. and France and members will be all the nations of the Middle East. In effect, a regional bloc will be formed in the same manner as the Helsinki Convention which helped disintegrate the Soviet Union.

To further the plan, Dr. Gold flew to Paris and met secretly with Senator Arlen Spector of the CFR who, afterward flew to Damascus with a message to Assad from Gold. Spector is long remembered as the member of the Warren Commission who devised the magic bullet theory to whitewash the assassination of President Kennedy. He is now among a long list of Jews including Kissinger, Clinton's Middle East envoy Dennis Ross, and American ambassador to Israel Martin Indyk, whose role is to make the weakening of Israel more palatable to American and Israeli Jews.

Prime Minister Netanyahu has accepted the new reality. When in opposition, he opposed the creation of a working group headed by France and the U.S. to oversee the cease-fire in Lebanon agreed to after Operation Grapes of Wrath. By August, he approved the formation of the group. While head of the opposition, he mocked Shimon Peres' promotion of a Middle East regional bank as part of the string of delusions Peres called the New Middle East. In July, he asked Congress to fund such a bank.

And as leader of the opposition, Netanyahu claimed to despise the Oslo channel led by Mr. and Mrs. Terje Larsen, the Norwegian couple who brought Arafat and Rabin together in "peace." Yet on August 14 at a secret meeting in the couple's Tel Aviv apartment attended by the PLO's diplomatic "minister" Abu Mazen, Gold, and David Bar Ilan, the infamous handshake between Netanyahu and Arafat was arranged.

Sometime after the meeting Gold made a bizarre confession to Dennis Ross. "If I was in the Holocaust," he said, "I would have liked to have hidden in the Larsen's basement." Yes, he really said that.

Bar Ilan, who for three years wrote scathing editorials against the hidden diplomacy of Oslo, was so proud of his role in bringing Netanyahu and Arafat together that he released every detail of the meeting to David Makovsky, an advocate of the "peace process."

After the notorious handshaking ceremony was over, Netanyahu was off to Washington to meet with the President. He returned and sent Defense Minister Yitzhak Mordechai to a meeting with Arafat to discuss the best way to withdraw from Hebron.

It was Dore Gold who Netanyahu first sent to meet Arafat back in June. It was Gold who arranged a series of secret meetings in London between Netanyahu and the Jordanian royal family. And it is Gold who is behind the Kissinger channel to Syria. But what do we really know about him?

He was considered a rare right-winger during his long stay at the left-wing Jaffe Center for Strategic Studies at Tel Aviv University. He wrote a series of dry analyses for the *Jerusalem Post*, one of which caught Netanyahu's eye in 1991. Netanyahu invited him to be a delegate to the Madrid Conference on Middle East Peace shortly after. This was followed by a tenure at the Washington Center for Near East Studies, the same think-tank that graduated Yossi Beilin and Ehud Barak. His mentor at the time was Martin Indyk, who was conducting secret negotiations with Ambassador Itamar Rabinovitch to arrange an Israeli withdrawal from the Golan Heights. Gold returned to Israel and heaped praise on Kissinger in a series of *Jerusalem Post* articles.

Gold and Indyk are now a team in Israel, which assures that the New World Order is controlling the diplomacy of the Netanyahu government.

More New World Order Developments

While Netanyahu and Gold sponsor the New World Order agenda, other Likud luminaries are also doing their part.

September 20 saw the publication in both *Kol Hair* and *Yerushalayim* of extended articles about Ehud Olmert's approval of a plan for dividing Jerusalem. The plan was developed by the Jerusalem Center for Israeli Studies and is a variation of previous plans promoted by Yossi Beilin and Teddy Kollek, both of whom gave their blessings to the new program.

The current attempt to divide the holy city has Jerusalem divided into Jewish secular, Jewish religious, and Arab sectors. Each sector oversees the municipal functions of thirty separate neighborhoods. While unwritten, the Arab sector will soon become the capital of a Palestinian state.

Until recently, Olmert could have acquiesced to the division of the city out of fear of legal action stemming from his involve-

ment in electoral fraud. However, by September he was indicted
and now faces an uphill battle to avoid prison. He reportedly
approved the new division plan after the indictment, so legal blackmail did not necessarily affect his decision.

The *Yerushalayim* headline read: "Olmert Will Divide Jerusalem," a play on the Likud election slogan, "Labor Will Divide
Jerusalem." Last April, *Haaretz* reported that Shimon Peres had
an angry outburst with Olmert over the slogan. "It's your plan, so
what do you want from me," he screamed at Olmert. No one
understood what he meant. Now it's clear.

In September Foreign Minister David Levy flew to Rome on
the same day as Yasser Arafat, who was to meet the pope. After
Levy met Italian Foreign Minister Umberto Dini, the pope cancelled his visit with Arafat, saying he was too busy preparing for
his trip to Hungary. His job done, Levy flew to Ireland to meet
another Catholic foreign minister, Jack Spring.

While the Italian intrigue took place, the Vatican in conjunc-
tion with the World Council of Churches led a conference in
Salonika, Greece, about the future of Jerusalem. The Israeli representative was David Forman, the government's agent to such hos-
tile religious organizations as Hamas and Islamic Jihad. Predictably, the conference issued a concluding statement demanding
that Israel liberalize its hold on the city.

While a select few Likud leaders are promoting new world
order agendas, most coalition and Likud members are being kept
blissfully in the dark. Menachem Rahat of *Maariv* reports, "Netanyahu is isolating himself from the Likud leadership, even refusing to give out his home phone number to the party faithful."
This has confused close aide Yvet Lieberman who complained to
Ariel Sharon, "I don't understand Bibi. I objected to his meeting
with Arafat and his plans to pull out of Hebron, but he doesn't
listen to me anymore." More and more as he promotes the New
World Order agenda, Netanyahu is becoming totally isolated from
the party he was given the mandate to lead.

Labor Update

Immediately after the May elections, Israel Radio reported that Shimon Peres and Binyamin Netanyahu began negotiations to form a unity government. In the end it was Peres who rejected the plan because "Netanyahu insisted on appointing Ehud Barak as his foreign minister."

But the negotiations continued through August, according to *Haaretz* and *Maariv*, between Ariel Sharon and Peres. According to *Maariv* reporter Orly Azulai-Katz, Sharon was acting under pressure from members of Shas, who were persuaded to lobby for a unity government by Ehud Barak.

The same reporter recently wrote a book about the failure of Peres to win the elections. Her main and perhaps only revelation was that Yitzhak Rabin had promised President Clinton a complete withdrawal from the Golan Heights to the pre-1967 borders. This tidbit was supplied to her by Peres which had some observers wondering why he chose to blacken Rabin's reputation at this point.

In August, Dore Gold revealed that the Labor government had "signed agreements with the PLO that endangered the state." The statement led some members of Knesset to demand that all the secret clauses of Oslo be made public.

In reaction, Yossi Beilin mounted a campaign to force Gold to retract his remarks. Within two days he did so. However, barely a week later, Oslo negotiator Yair Hirschfeld told both Army Radio and the settler magazine *Nativ* that had Labor won, his and Beilin's agreement with the PLO would have gone into effect. Among the results would have been a Palestinian state with a suburb of Jerusalem as its capital and a total withdrawal from the Jordan valley.Beilin initially refused to comment on Hirschfeld's unexpected revelations of his illegal diplomatic activities, but finally had no choice but to acknowledge their veracity. To protect himself, he announced that he would run for the party leadership on the secret deal's platform.

Bits and Pieces

- One of the proofs that Washington was behind the first Oslo Accord was Rabin's supposed choice of a Washington lawyer and longtime Israeli emigre Yoel Zinger to write the agreement. Zinger denied such suspicions, saying he was an Israeli who had come home, not a front for Washington's direct involvement in the "peace" process. Well, in August, his job done and the damage permanent, Zinger moved back to Washington permanently.
- One has to wonder why the government overreacted to an article in a harmless tourist newspaper called *The Traveller*. It arrested writer David Ben Ariel, jailed him for a week, then deported him. Ben Ariel's piece was called, "Will Jerusalem Become an International City?" and described a Vatican-German plot to take over the Temple Mount in the Old City. Editor Nick Day was a bit perplexed by the seriousness of the government's response. "David Ben-Ariel was a nice non-Jewish guy with a great love for this country," he noted.
- Hugo Asfania, an Ecuadorian police officer, is worrying his counterparts in Israel. He published a book claiming an Israeli policeman, Ran Gazit, trained Ecuadorian officers in the fine art of torturing prisoners.
- *Yediot Achronot* (August 14, 1996) claims, based on a close reading of this year's *Jane's Guide*, that Jonathan Pollard's intelligence unit, AL, is still operating in the U.S. and to protect its activities, Pollard's deserved release from prison is being delayed, perhaps permanently.
- Four months after his suspicious disappearance, the chief engineer of the Dimona nuclear reactor, Yaron Daniel, is still missing and nobody knows where to find him. And still the government will not admit that its nuclear secrets have been deeply compromised.
- According to the *Washington Times*, Dennis Ross is on the way out and will be replaced by Richard Holbrooke as the President's

Middle East envoy. Holbrooke's last assignment was to place thousands of U.N. troops in Bosnia.

- The large-circulation Moscow daily *Svodnia* reports that "Yasser Arafat is one of the world's leading Mafia godfathers who has personally amassed $12 billion selling arms and drugs." The paper adds, "While small-time drug and weapons smugglers languish in prison endlessly, Arafat leads the Palestinian people and has turned the autonomous regions into an international center for illegal trafficking of arms and narcotics."

- Israeli papers have suddenly become no less critical of the PLO. Ehud Yaari, the pro-peace commentator, notes that corruption and violence have become so intolerable that Arab leaders in Hebron have appealed to the IDF not to withdraw from the city. Khalad Abu-Tuoma, an Arab reporter for *Yerushalayim*, reports that PLO "policemen" are torturing Palestinians with dual Israeli citizenship. Yaacov Galatni of *Yediot Achronot* writes that Israeli Arabs are smuggling funds to help the family of a terrorist who planned operations that killed over sixty Jews. The far left *Kol Hair* reports that Zakhi Nakhas, deputy mayor of Albira, has been held and tortured for three weeks by the PLO's intelligence force for the crime of being appointed by the Israeli-established municipal council. The same paper reports that Arafat has set up the headquarters for Shabiba, his "national" youth organization, in Jerusalem, while *Haaretz* writer Eitan Rabin writes that the PLO's security apparatus is working out of over one hundred apartments in Area C, in contravention of the Cairo Accord of last year.

- Agent provocateur Avishai Raviv lied at the trial of the two Kahalani brothers, who were wrongly convicted of attempted murder after being trapped in a Shabak sting operation and sentenced to twelve years each. Without an ounce of irony in his voice, Raviv testified that he didn't work for the Shabak and the judge raised no objections. However, Eli Goldin was charged with basically the same crime, but received only four months because his lawyer charged Raviv with setting up his client and demanded that he testify. The judge reduced the sentence on condition that Raviv stay out of his courtroom.

- The Deri trial is finally dragging in some big fish. Defense witness Moshe Weinberg testified that in 1986, then-Prime Minister Shimon Peres agreed to exchange some worthless land purchased by Arye Deri's real estate concern for prime government property on Har Shmuel. A lot on the new property was offered to London real estate magnate Martin Brown who sued Deri for fraud. Brown, reports Edna Adito of *Yediot Achronot,* "is terrified of some kind of revenge by Deri." Also presented at the Deri trial was a tape of Weinberg secretly recorded in 1995 saying that the Shabak had given him a list of all Shas party members being bugged by the force.

- In another tell-all book about Labor's loss at the polls, authors Ben Caspit and Ilan Kfir reveal that President Clinton directly aided Peres by secretly sending his polling expert Douglas Shawn to Israel to help him win the elections.

- A major piece of NWO news that received little attention was the U.N.'s decision on July 15 to move the headquarters of its relief organization UNRWA from Vienna to Gaza, of all places. So far there is no media reaction from the bureaucrats who were forced to give up Europe for the squalor of the Gaza Strip.

- Why is it that every time Germany plots its hidden agenda with Israel, the public is told the real reason for high level meetings is to liberate Ron Arad, the air force navigator who was downed in Lebanon a decade ago? When Peres flew to Germany and met with its foreign minister in April, the purpose of the meeting was announced to be the recovery of Arad from an Iranian jail. In August the German defense minister arrived in Israel for three days of talks, all supposedly in the interest of Ron Arad.

- According to the Brazilian daily *Vega,* in one of his more bizarre plots, in 1994 Shimon Peres offered the Brazilian government a deal. In return for freeing an Israeli model imprisoned there for trying to smuggle an allegedly illegally adopted baby out of the country, he would release PLO terrorist Lamia Maruf from her

Israeli prison. Which begs the question, why would Brazil be interested in the release of a Palestinian terrorist?

- Publicly, Bank of Israel chief Yaacov Frenkel is the model of judicious spending, supposedly opposed to the government borrowing money abroad. Yet according to Gideon Eshet of *Yediot Achronot*, "In 1991 Frenkel travelled to Washington to persuade the American government to offer Israel $10 billion in guarantees to borrow money from commercial banks." This is in keeping with World Bank policies to indebt nations into compliance with IMF recovery programs.

Chapter 10

January 1997

The Mad Rush to Unity

The Likud coalition is sitting securely in the Knesset with sixty-seven seats, yet after four years in the political wilderness top party members are pushing hard for a unity government with Labor. If this desire isn't inexplicable in itself, it becomes more so when one considers that the prime movers are two right-wing ideologues, Ariel Sharon and party chairman Michael Eitan.

There are two unity tracks. The first, led by Sharon, wants Shimon Peres back in government. Eitan is pushing Yossi Beilin and leading a movement to have his secret deal with the PLO's Abu Mazen accepted as the basis for a final agreement with the Palestinian Authority. What or who is behind the mad rush to unity?

The Peres Channel

In the case of Sharon, the answer is Henry Kissinger. In early October, President Hosni Mubarak invited Sharon to a three-way meeting with Peres in Cairo. On October 17 Sharon met with Kissinger at what was supposed to be a secret meeting at the Sheraton Hotel in Manhattan. Sharon was attending an economic conference at the hotel and took pains to have the meeting in a hidden room. However, he and Kissinger were spotted by reporters who later peppered him with questions at a press conference.

In reply to a journalist inquiring about the peace process, Sharon surprised him by explaining, "There must be sacrifices for peace. Peace, like war, is cruel. It requires concessions." When asked if he meant territorial concessions, Sharon did not answer.

Following his meeting with Kissinger, Sharon cancelled his

Cairo meeting with Peres, preferring to initiate a series of semi-secret meetings with him at his home in Ramat Aviv. He described the meetings as "social encounters." The day following the Kissinger-Sharon meeting, *Inside Israel* phoned Sharon's spokesman, Raanan Giffin. He was asked why the meeting took place.

"I don't know why everyone is making such a fuss about it. Mr. Sharon has met Dr. Kissinger every time he's flown to America over the past twenty-five years."

What was discussed at this meeting? "Where the peace process with the Palestinians is going and overall regional peace issues."

Why would the minister of infrastructure discuss peace issues at an economic conference? "You're right. They discussed promoting infrastructure projects."

Did the minister cancel his Cairo meeting with Mubarak at Kissinger's request? "You're not the first to imply such a thing. It's just not true. Mr. Sharon cancelled the meeting before he met with Dr. Kissinger."

Why have they been meeting over the past twenty-five years? "Dr. Kissinger and Mr. Sharon have shared a deep friendship that began after the Yom Kippur War."

The issue I'm particularly interested in is Dr. Kissinger's stewardship of the Council on Foreign Relations. Would it be possible to arrange a meeting with Mr. Sharon to discuss the issue? "Mr. Sharon has instructed me not to publicize his diplomatic activities until the time is right."

Will that be soon? "I'll inform you when he is ready."

Until that day, Sharon and Peres are busy plotting the latter's return to power within the Netanyahu government, undoubtedly with Kissinger's powerful blessing.

Michael Eitan Changes Course

In opposition, Michael Eitan was one of the most vigorous opponents of the Oslo Accords. Now in power, he has been organizing fellow Likud Knesset members to back perhaps the most dastardly of the secret post-Oslo agreements. Last March Yossi Beilin and the PLO's "foreign minister" Abu Mazen concluded a final treaty between Israel and the Palestinian Authority.

The main points were that a Palestinian state would emerge with its capital being the Jerusalem suburb of Abu Dis. There would be a corridor linking Abu Dis with the Temple Mount which would be under PLO control. In return for keeping settlements intact under Palestinian control, Israel would give up large chunks of land in the Negev Desert to expand the Gaza Strip. Israel would also give up control of the Jordan Valley in return for maintaining a chain of isolated fortresses along the river.

This is the agreement Michael Eitan is pushing as a basis for a final settlement with the Palestinian Authority. In October he announced, "The time has come for a national unity government," and no analyst could properly explain Eitan's behavior. However, he quickly succeeded in luring some most unexpected advocates to his cause. According to Ben Caspit writing in *Yediot Achronot*, "High ranking Knesset and Prime Minister's Office officials are studying the understanding reached between Yossi Beilin and Abu Mazen last year. One minister said, 'We can certainly live with part of the principles of this plan.'"

Names of Beilin's co-plotters were revealed by Sarah Friedman of *Maariv*, who was leaked a copy of Beilin's secret note inviting MK Uzi Baram to join the conspiracy. It read: "Michael Eitan and I agreed to organize a meeting of Likud and Labor MKs to prepare a joint plan for a final settlement. I suggested that our side be represented by Ephraim Sneh, [Haim] Ramon, [Shlomo] Ben Ami, and you. Do you want to join? If so, signal me and I'll understand." Ben Caspit reported that Baram agreed and was later joined by former finance minister Avraham Shohat.

Bibi's Role
All this secret activity is not going on behind Prime Minister

Netanyahu's back. He has held his own meetings with Gesher MK Yehuda Harel and Meretz head Yossi Sarid to discuss a national unity government, a subject that should be the last thing on his mind.

But the most revealing hint of Netanyahu's intentions came from the lips of Arye Deri, the Shas head, now on trial for massive fraud and embezzlement. After his meeting wih Abu Mazen at the home of Yossi Ginnosar in Kochav Yair was exposed, Deri explained, "The prime minister pressured me to have this meeting to arrange another meeting between Arafat and Rabbi Ovadia Yosef on his behalf."

Also attending the meeting was Deri's sometime business crony Haim Ramon. Rabbi Ovadia Yosef is the spiritual leader of Shas and his endorsement of the Beilin-Abu Mazen deal would sway the Moroccan community towards acceptance of it. As for Ginnosar, former Prime Minister Yitzhak Rabin tried appointing him to high office but was forced to rescind any nomination because of Ginnosar's shady past. To cover up his role in a deadly IDF fiasco during the Lebanon War, Ginnosar perjured himself to a military court, resulting in the wrongful sentencing of a Druze IDF officer.

These are the folks Netanyahu has chosen to promote a unity government dedicated to reaching a final agreement with the PLO based on secret and deceitful negotiations between Beilin and Abu Mazen last year. Lest anyone ask why, much of the answer lies in an equally secret and deceitful meeting between Sharon and Kissinger on October 17.

Christian and Jewish Holy Sites Desecrated

In the wake of last September's bloody skirmishes supposedly ignited by the opening of a tunnel to the Temple Mount, Jerusalem mayor Ehud Olmert revealed a secret understanding reached by the previous government and the Moslem governing council

(Wakf). During the month-long Ramadan holiday, El Aqsa mosque could no longer accommodate the throngs of worshipers. The Wakf asked the Israelis to allow the cavernous underground site, Solomon's Stables, to be used as a prayer station for the overflow crowd. Israel agreed in return for no opposition to opening the later contentious tunnel.

Solomon's Stables, whose entrance is below Damascus Gate, was the main quarry used for supplying stone to Solomon's Temple. As the stone was removed from what was a small cave, an underground labyrinth was created. Crusader invaders during the eleventh century turned the cavern into a large stable, thus its current misnomer.

After the Ramadan season was over, the Wakf abused Israel's favor and began expanding the temporary mosque. This year a decision was made to build a permanent structure in Solomon's Stables. By doing so, the Wakf knowingly planned to desecrate holy sites to Judaism and Christianity. Moslem religious leaders are certainly aware that the site was created by Jewish stone masons three thousand years ago. For that reason, plus the later building of the Crusader stables by the Knights of Malta and Templar Knights, Solomon's Stables are also a pilgrimage destination for Freemasons. What they may or may not have known is the site of their new mosque may well be on the ancient Holy of Holies.

At least that's what Tel Aviv architect Tuvia Saguy is claiming. After seven years of research, Saguy has located the Holy of Holies sixteen meters under the Temple Mount, almost precisely in the middle of the new mosque.

If his claim is contentious, that of the Christians is not. The Wakf is planning to rip down a marble shrine called the Cradle of Jesus. Here, Christians believe, Jesus was nursed by Mary after he was forty days old.

In an eyes-only memo sent by Police Inspector Arieh Amit to Interior Security Minister Avigdor Kahalani and leaked to *Yediot Achronot*, Amit writes," I have received information that the Wakf is going to destroy the Cradle. The result would be not merely a great archaeological loss, there is a grave danger of an eruption of hostilities between Moslems and Christians."

Archaeologist Meir Den-Dov agrees. "Any destruction of Jesus' Cradle would be a source of bitter conflict between Moslems and Christians."

Secret PA Memo Found

Ruby Steiner of Alfei-Menashe was surprised to find a message in Arabic sent to her fax machine. Apparently, the sender misdialed or there was a technical glitch. However it happened, Steiner received a top secret memo from the head of the Palestinian Secret Services, Muhmad Dakhlan, to the director-general of Yasser Arafat's office, Dr. Ramzi Khouri. The memo makes interesting reading. Among the points are an analysis of Dennis Ross' sympathy for the Israeli negotiating position, followed by advice to exploit Jacques Chirac's upcoming visit to bring Europe into the picture as a counterbalance to the U.S. That makes Chirac's boorish behavior toward Israel more logical in retrospect. This is followed by a list of Israeli negotiating positions over Hebron that would be opposed, such as no buildings over three stories within a 150 meter radius of the Jewish Quarter.

But the most significant discovery is an analysis of the IDF's fighting mood in light of the September battles. The memo reads:

Re: The El Aqsa War [The PLO's name for the battles]—Low and middle ranking Israeli officers are feeling very humiliated since the events and a mood of revenge has erupted among them. In interviews, many are speaking of a Palestinian victory, especially in Nablus. Thus, many are waiting for a second round to recover their pride. I recommend a policy of restraint to protect our gains, locally and internationally. In Washington and elsewhere, we have received unprecedented support.

If there is shame in the IDF, much is warranted. During the siege of Joseph's Tomb in Nablus, two armored patrol carriers were sent to rescue ten soldiers within the shrine. Their officer, sticking to a strict interpretation of the Cairo "peace" treaty, ordered his soldiers to keep the doors of their vehicles open and not to open fire at snipers. As a direct result, six young Israelis were slaughtered in their APCs. Joseph's Tomb then became the tomb of two more IDF soldiers killed when rioters led by Palestinian Authority policemen shooting their Israeli-issued automatic rifles, overran the site. It was burnt and Jewish holy books were desecrated and destroyed.

A photographer captured the pathetic moment when an IDF soldier begged for his life. It was quickly distributed throughout the Palestinian communities. The caption underneath the photo in one Palestinian paper read, "Israeli Soldier Crying Like a Baby."

In a typical reaction, on the day following the battle, the *Voice of Palestine* interviewed a nearby resident. "This was an unforgettable day in Palestinian history," he recounted. "Our brave *fedayeen*, heroes of the intifada, really put it to the Israeli enemy. They set two jeeps on fire and took two others which they drove around Nablus in glory. It was an emotional moment."

Needless to say, Israeli intelligence believes the image of the IDF soldier has been deeply tarnished and this will encourage more attacks against military targets.

The Latest in American Grooming Habits

In October 1996, Syria conducted a large military exercise near the Golan Heights. To allay Israeli fears of an impending attack they sent the following message to Secretary of State Warren Christopher to be relayed to the Israeli ambassador to Washington, Benjamin Ben Elisar: "Syria has no intention to going to war against Israel. Our maneuvers are purely a defensive exercise to prevent a surprise attack."

Christopher told Ben Elisar that the Syrians were preparing
for war that would break out unless there was progress in the
peace negotiations. Ben Elisar fumed at the threat and relayed it
to Jerusalem. The IDF went on alert and the threat of war was in
the air.

Maariv's Ben Caspit reports that when Syria was informed of
Christopher's lie, President Assad decided he could no longer trust
Washington as a go-between. Why did Christopher lie? Clearly
the maneuver was aimed at heating up the region and it could
have easily led to full scale war. Ben Caspit concludes that this
was Washington's way of prodding the Netanyahu government
into serious peace talks. Other analysts believe that Washington
actually wanted to ignite a war. Journalist Nahum Barnea writes:

> America is back grooming ministers to oppose the prime min-
> ister from within. During Begin's time, they groomed Dayan,
> Weizman, and Aharon Barak. The fruits of the effort were the
> Camp David Accords. In Shamir's time they groomed Meridor,
> Olmert, Levy, and Milo. The result was the Madrid Conference.
> Currently, they are busy grooming Levy, President Weizman,
> and Defense Minister Yitzhak Mordecai.

Indeed, they are. During Mordecai's October visit to America, he
was flown to Washington from New York on Hillary Clinton's
private jet where a full-blown sirens-wailing motorcade drove him
to the White House. One Israeli observer was nonplussed: "Why
all the fuss? They usually reserve this kind of treatment for visiting royalty."

The grooming may not be as necessary with Netanyahu as
with his predecessors. According to *Haaretz*, during the prime
minister's August visit to Washington, he promised the President
that no new building would take place in the territories without
the consent of the U.S., Jordan, and Egypt.

About the Author

In 1992, Canongate Publishers of Edinburgh, published Barry Chamish's book *The Fall of Israel*, which contended that internal political corruption was endangering Israel's existence. Shortly after the book's publication, Mr. Chamish co-founded the intelligence newsletter *Inside Israel*. Mr. Chamish's articles have appeared in hundreds of publications, including *The Atlantic*, *New York Newsday*, and *The National Review*. He lives in Bet Shemesh, Israel, with his wife and two children.